Beauty Is
SOUL DEEP
180 devotionals

for growing a

meaningful inner life

COMPILED AND EDITED BY

JUNE HETZEL AND MICHELLE LEE

BARBOUR

PUBLISHING

WITH DEEP APPRECIATION TO...

Geoffrey O. Hetzel, husband
Stella Ma, friend
Debbie Graham, friend
Deborah McIntire, friend
Shannon Hill, editor

. . .for your support in developing this project.

© 2003 by Barbour Publishing, Inc.

ISBN 1-59310-017-5

Cover image © GettyOne

Published by Barbour Publishing, Inc., P.O. Box 719, Uhrichsville, Ohio 44683, www.barbourbooks.com. Our mission is to publish and distribute inspirational products offering exceptional value and biblical encouragement to the masses.

Member of the
Evangelical Christian
Publishers Association

Printed in the United States of America.

Dear Reader,

Have you ever wondered, *Do I look okay? Will people like me? Am I normal? Will I fit in?* Have you ever felt insecure? lonely? confused? We have. And, if you have, you are not alone. Young women around the world experience these same types of thoughts and feelings.

Young and old, women want to be beautiful and they want to be loved. However, sometimes they feel insecure about their looks, their personality, or their relationships. This is what this collection of devotionals is all about. . .how to become a woman of *real* beauty, how to gain confidence, how to become genuine in your friendships, and how to gain a deeper understanding that you are unconditionally loved by the Lord Jesus Christ. His desire is for you to get to know Him better and become more like Him—this creates *genuine* beauty.

Journey with us through *Beauty Is Soul Deep: 180 Devotionals for Growing a Meaningful Inner Life.* Talk with famous and influential singers and models, authors and artists, athletes and missionaries, moms and daughters, teens and teachers. Listen to the wisdom of Rebecca St. James, Mother Teresa, Shirley Dobson, Elisabeth Elliott, Misty Bernall, Barbara Johnson, Joni Eareckson Tada, and others. Hear these women discuss what really matters most. Find out that they too have struggled with feelings of insecurity that could be overcome only by the transforming work of our Lord Jesus Christ.

As you walk with us through this journey, prayerfully read at least one devotional each day and discover what beauty is all about. Laugh with us and cry with us, but most importantly, be open to the Holy Spirit's teaching, for it is His character that will create true beauty in you.

Praying that you'll be blessed by this book,

JUNE AND MICHELLE
Beauty Is Soul Deep editors
November 2003

REAL BEAUTY

Heather Whitestone McCallum,
former Miss America,
with Angela Hunt

> *"For if you remain silent at this time, relief and
> deliverance for the Jews will arise from another place,
> but you and your father's family will perish.
> And who knows but that you have come
> to royal position for such a time as this?"*
>
> ESTHER 4:14 NIV

I always read in the Bible about how important our heart is to God, and I believe that beauty from the heart is what brings glory to God. When I hear people talk about how beautiful I am, I often feel embarrassed. I want to be more beautiful on the inside than on the outside. Sometimes I wish I were kinder and gentler and more giving—that's real beauty.

As the story of Esther demonstrates, the world is filled with beautiful women, but women who are filled with courage, faith, and devotion will rise above the rest. You can be an Esther too. Even when you feel your dreams have crumbled to dust, you can turn to the God who made you and loves you and trust Him to bring you up from the ashes clothed in honor, confidence, and glory.

Let God surprise you with beauty—where you least expect it.

I AM VALUABLE

Tonya Ruiz,
author of *Beauty Quest—A Model's Journey*

> *But God demonstrates His own love toward us,*
> *in that while we were still sinners, Christ died for us.*
>
> ROMANS 5:8 NKJV

At age sixteen, I moved to Paris and became a fashion model. My rail-thin body, shiny blond hair, and sky blue eyes were my passport to wealth and fame. *TEEN Magazine* wrote an article about my life—"Model Success Story." It was like something that happened in the movies.

Life was one big party. It never occurred to me that my excessive eating and drinking could affect how I looked, but they did. I looked puffy and tired. I became consumed with the way I looked. When I scrutinized my appearance, it was like looking in a fun house mirror. My view was distorted—what was real was not what I saw. I put my personal value in the way I looked, and since I could not always look perfect, I felt worthless.

When I became a Christian, I learned that physical beauty is only skin-deep and temporary, but that true beauty is soul deep. God accepts me regardless of my jean size, the condition of my skin, or my reflection in a mirror. He loves me so much that He sent His only Son to die for me. I am, indeed, deeply loved by God and valuable to Him.

GUESS WHO

Martha Bolton,
writer

There are different kinds of gifts, but the same Spirit.
There are different kinds of service, but the same Lord.
There are different kinds of working, but the same
God works all of them in all men.

1 CORINTHIANS 12:4–6 NIV

Have you ever tried to solve one of those puzzles where they've made a single face out of several different celebrities? It might be Brad Pitt's nose, Bruce Willis's ears, Ray Romano's chin, and so on. The finished product barely looks human, and it's your job to figure out which facial part belongs to which celebrity.

Sometimes that's what we try doing with our own identities. We're a little bit of this person and little more of that person over there. We add a dash of him and scoop of her, and by the time we're finished, there's very little of us left in the picture.

When God created us, He designed us to be unique individuals, not clones of someone else. He didn't want us to look, act, think, sing, draw, write, play an instrument, or do anything exactly like someone else. We each have our own distinct personalities. We each have our own desires, goals, and dreams. We each have our own talents. We each have our own passion. We each have our own life. God has a custom-designed plan for each one of us, but it's up to us to follow it.

Liz on Looks

Liz, high school student, West Chester, Ohio
Written by Krishana Kraft of *Brio*

*Charm is deceitful and beauty is vain, but a woman
who fears the Lord, she shall be praised.*

PROVERBS 31:30 NASB

Constantly I hear about another girl at my school or church who is struggling with an eating disorder. Even if she hasn't taken it to an extreme level, it's still a major concern.

We all desire to have confidence in ourselves. But many girls believe they can only have confidence in themselves with a thin physique, which is how an eating disorder can start.

I wish girls would understand how God views them and would place all their confidence in Him. Then girls might not struggle with eating disorders and so many other heartbreaking things. I'm convinced that the best cure would be placing all of our happiness and joy in Christ instead of in ourselves.

A verse that I came across recently was Proverbs 31:30 (NIV), "Charm is deceptive, and beauty is fleeting; but a woman who fears the LORD is to be praised." God continues to teach me that fearing Him is essential. It's the key to true beauty!

Having the right attitude of reverent fear toward God is the only way I'll receive His best for me in life. He is most glorified when I'm most satisfied in Him.

BEAUTY IS SOUL DEEP

BEYOND COMPARISON

Nancy C. Anderson,
conference and retreat speaker

*They are only comparing themselves with each other,
and measuring themselves by themselves.
What foolishness!*

2 CORINTHIANS 10:12 NLT

I *wish I was as pretty as Juli. I wish I was as funny as Chelsea. I wish I was as smart as Jessica,* I thought as I passed each of those girls in the hallway. I was constantly comparing myself to others, and I never measured up.

I thought, *Their lives seem so wonderful and mine is so ordinary. They must know a secret that I don't know.* So, I decided to ask them about their "perfect" lives, and I found out that *they* were comparing themselves to other people too.

Juli, who was short, said that she wished she could be tall like me. Chelsea said that the reason she told so many jokes was to keep up with her sister, who was funnier than *she* was. And Jessica said that she got straight A's just to please her father, who was a genius and yelled at her if she got a B.

That's when I decided to stop comparing myself to other people and try instead to be more like Jesus, who is kind, compassionate, and loving beyond comparison.

GROW IN GRACE

Joni Eareckson Tada,
quadriplegic writer and speaker

And we, who with unveiled faces
all reflect the Lord's glory,
are being transformed into his likeness
with ever-increasing glory.

2 CORINTHIANS 3:18 NIV

I received a letter from an old school friend the other day. After twenty-five years of friendship, it was good to read that she is still growing in the Lord. But I was especially touched with her closing salutation, "Grow in grace." It made me think: *Just how have I grown in God's grace over the last year? Is this something that can be measured?*

Bishop J. C. Ryle puts it this way: "When I speak of a person growing in grace, I mean simply this—that his sense of sin is becoming deeper, his faith stronger, his hope brighter, his love more extensive, and his spiritual-mindedness more marked. He feels more of the power of godliness in his heart. He manifests more of it in his life. He goes on from strength to strength, from faith to faith, and from grace to grace."

We can be transformed into His likeness; something fundamentally different can happen in our lives from year to year. Change is possible, and a new and improved you is within reach. This is how it happens: Behold the Lord's glory, and you will grow in grace.

DYING TO BE THIN

Tonya Ruiz,
author of *Beauty Quest—A Model's Journey*

"For the Lord sees not as man sees;
for man looks on the outward appearance,
but the Lord looks on the heart."

1 SAMUEL 16:7 AMP

At age sixteen, I was a 120-pound fashion model who was always on a diet. After a weeklong fast, I went to see my agent. She said, "You're still fat, lose five more pounds." That night, I defiantly ate a box of frosted flakes and then swallowed a handful of laxatives and diet pills. Finally, I sat with my head over a toilet trying to make myself vomit. I started skipping meals and lost weight. I got down to 108 pounds, and my new thinner image was in magazines, commercials, and on billboards. I was literally dying to be thin.

Two years later, at age eighteen, I became a Christian and walked away from the modeling business. I slowly realized the scale was no longer my enemy. By reading the Bible, I learned that God was more concerned about the spiritual condition of my heart than my physical appearance.

NEITHER HERE NOR THERE

Martha Bolton,
writer

*You adulterous people, don't you know that friendship
with the world is hatred toward God?
Anyone who chooses to be a friend of the world
becomes an enemy of God.*

JAMES 4:4 NIV

There's a place here in America called Four Corners. It's where four of our states—Arizona, New Mexico, Utah, and Colorado—all meet. You can stand at a certain spot and have one foot in New Mexico, one in Arizona, a hand in Utah, and your other hand in Colorado. A family of four can have each family member in a different state and still hug each other. You can eat a sandwich in New Mexico, then have dessert in Utah seconds later. As you can see, Four Corners is a fun place to visit.

When it comes to spiritual matters, we're supposed to be a lot more stable than that. We can't be for God in one place, like church, then take a few steps to another place, like school, and deny Him. We can't be for everything He stands for on Sunday, then be against everything He stands for by Wednesday. God wants our faith to be consistent.

In other words, you might be able to have your feet and hands in four different states at the same time, but you can't have four different views of faith and be left standing on any true convictions.

FROM THE INSIDE OUT

Durlynn Anema-Garten,
Christian counselor

Your beauty should not come from outward adornment,
such as braided hair and the wearing of gold jewelry and fine clothes.
Instead, it should be that of your inner self, the unfading beauty
of a gentle and quiet spirit, which is of great worth in God's sight.

1 PETER 3:3–4 NIV

"**T**rue beauty comes from inside." I often heard these words from my grandmother, but I rarely listened.

Instead, I paid heed to the women who received the most attention—ones the world considered beautiful—women with perfect facial features, curvy bodies, lustrous hair, small noses. They were my image of beauty when I was a teenager—until I was in a medical lab for a blood test.

The older lady in the next cubicle smiled and said hello. She sensed I was nervous and evidently wanted to calm me. She told me she had a miserable time getting out of bed that morning. She explained she had two knee replacements, plus arthritis so crippling she could hardly move.

As she talked, I kept looking at her face. It was radiant. Every facial feature glowed—smooth skin, bright eyes, larger than average nose. I couldn't resist telling her how beautiful she was.

She smiled, then said, "Thank you, but it's not me. It's the Lord. He helps me every minute of every day—so why not be peaceful and grateful?"

"And radiant," I added to myself. That's when I learned that beauty does come from inside.

BLUE IS BECOMING

Twila Paris,
recording artist

Sing for joy in the LORD, O you righteous ones;
Praise is becoming to the upright.

PSALM 33:1 NASB

When I was a little girl, my grandmother told me that the color blue was becoming to me because I had blue eyes. She simply meant that I looked good in blue, and it's a funny thing—I still wear blue an awful lot!

So when I read in the Bible that "praise is becoming to the upright," I was struck by the thought that we as Christians are actually more beautiful when we worship. Of course this Scripture is referring to spiritual beauty, but I've noticed that it shines through. More than once, I have looked around the room during worship and noticed faces that most people would consider plain looking positively radiant as they poured out their love and worship to the Father. And I've thought to myself, *If praise is this beautiful on the outside to my human eyes, how much more beautiful it must be on the inside to the eyes of a loving God.*

TRUST GOD'S LEADING

Debrah Jay Smith,
Young Life area director,
Huntington Beach, California

Trust GOD from the bottom of your heart;
don't try to figure out everything on your own.
Listen for GOD's voice in everything you do, everywhere you go;
he's the one who will keep you on track.

PROVERBS 3:5–6 THE MESSAGE

I recently took a trip to Catalina Island for the specific purpose of having a day alone. As I settled on the beach, eager to meet with God—and be met by Him—I witnessed an incredible sight. A little girl was lost. She seemed scared, shaken, confused, and disoriented. Her eyes were darting in every direction as she tried to locate either Mom or Dad.

Her search ended when she looked out past her immediate surroundings and found her father. I watched as, without hesitation, she ran full-force toward him. He embraced her. . .equally grateful to see she was safe. Just then, with arms extended, he took his daughter's trembling hands in his. With eyes of joy, she looked up and stepped softly atop his shoes. The two began to dance. He led. She followed. . .unrestrained, confident, and trusting His leading.

Being a teenager is tough. At times you feel disoriented, confused, or even a little lost. But, just past your immediate surroundings, God is waiting to lead you through the chaos. As you step atop God's feet, He will shift your fear into faith and your doubts into courage. Let His voice be that which guides you.

WHAT ARE YOU WORTH?

Angela Risley,
student,
Oklahoma Christian University

> *How many are your works, O LORD!*
> *In wisdom you made them all.*
>
> PSALM 104:24 NIV

How much money do you spend on buying clothes? How about jewelry or shoes? Most everyone enjoys looking nice and showing off her best appearance. I have a friend who doesn't leave her house until her "face is on" or until her makeup is perfect. There is something in us that almost demands that we give a great impression to those around us.

That's just it. We're trying to impress the wrong people and going about it the wrong way. Women of all ages complain: "I'm too short." "I'm too fat." "My nose is too big." Instead of concentrating on how much the "right look" is worth, we should be focusing on how beautiful we are simply because we are children of God.

God doesn't care about our outward appearances. He already thinks we're magnificent because He made us perfectly. When we're not so busy prettying up our outsides, we can look more closely at our inner selves. It is then that we can finally realize not how much our outer image is worth to us, but how much our inner beauty is worth to God.

WHAT CAN I DO?

Rebecca St. James,
recording artist

How, then, can they call on the one they have not believed in?
And how can they believe in the one of whom they have not heard?
And how can they hear without someone preaching to them?

ROMANS 10:14–15 NIV

Remember when you were a kid and people asked you, "What are you going to do when you grow up?" Well, I really don't believe that we have to be "grown up" to be used by God. God is God, and He can use whomever He wants—no matter how young. I think as teenagers we need to be using these years to do God's will and make a difference. We are part of a generation He is calling to be sold out for Him.

In Australia, only five percent of the population attends church, and being a Christian often draws a lot of negative attention. It's really black-and-white. If you're a believer in Jesus, people ask why you go to church.

God may be calling you to serve Him outside your country, or He may just want you to serve your friends and neighbors right where you live. He may call you to go on a foreign mission trip or just a daily mission trip in your neighborhood. The important thing is to bloom where you're planted.

WHAT AM I SUPPOSED TO DO?

Jennifer Knapp,
recording artist

> *"For whoever exalts himself will be humbled,*
> *and whoever humbles himself will be exalted."*
>
> MATTHEW 23:12 NIV

I have a friend who likes to use this phrase to catch people's attention: "If you want to know how to be humble, just read my latest book, *Humility and How I Attained It!*" Obviously he doesn't really mean it. However, it is so true that the subject of humility is a hard one to describe or even talk about.

I've found that one of the best symbolic positions of humility is getting on my knees. When I'm on my knees, I pray, I clean the places that are hard to get to, I plant seeds in the ground. On my knees I move around at a slower pace, and on my knees I always have to look up. Most of us don't spend a lot of time on our knees. Try it! It's a great way to learn more about humility.

Jesus makes the point that in order to become great, we must first learn to be humble—if we want to lead, we must first learn to serve. Jesus lived it out. He humbled Himself because His Father asked Him to. Your heavenly Father is asking you to do the same.

FOREVER LOVE

Lorraine Peterson,
writer

The LORD is compassionate and gracious, slow to anger,
abounding in love. . . . For as high as the heavens are above
the earth, so great is his love for those who fear him.

PSALM 103:8, 11 NIV

The Bible speaks often about God's "steadfast love."
Steadfast love is forever love. It never changes. It
is always the same.

God will always love you. Jesus came to earth to
offer visible proof of God's eternal love. Although
Jesus knew that the "rich young ruler" would not give
up his wealth to follow Him, the Bible says, "And Jesus
looking upon him loved him."

Jesus loved the woman with the bad reputation
who put perfume on His feet at a dinner party, and He
made her feel comfortable among the critical guests.
Jesus loved Thomas the doubter and did everything
possible to help him believe.

Jesus loves you and will demonstrate His love to
you—if you let Him. A person can accept love only
from someone he trusts. You can trust Jesus and
depend on Him for never-ending love.

DIETS

Kerry Stavert,
single parent of five

A false balance is abomination to the LORD,
but a just weight is his delight.

PROVERBS 11:1 KJV

Something about college inspires girls to look their best, particularly as far as their weight is concerned. Perhaps it is because we as women bond well in the kitchen, and that without a kitchen of our own, we substitute our dorm rooms and share diet tips. Instead of aprons and food preparation, we don flattering wardrobes and try various methods of food restriction.

I tried them all: the coffee diet, the grapefruit diet, the low-carb diet, the high-carb diet, the bran muffin and peanut butter diet, the smoothie diet. If the diet was there, I tried it. I never reached my goal for my ideal weight, and neither did my self-discipline or self-esteem improve.

In frustration, during my senior year, I came up with one last attempt to look great. I threw away my scale, focused on eating nutritious food in moderation, and let God do the rest. Guess what? I looked better than I ever did from any of my diets, and I felt great! As I sought to please God with how I ate, He gave me the added blessing of being pleased with myself.

IMPORTANT THINGS IN LIFE

Misty Bernall,
mother of teen martyr Cassie Bernall

*"Do not be worried about your life, as to what you will eat
or what you will drink; nor for your body, as to what you will put on.
Is not life more than food, and the body more than clothing?"*

MATTHEW 6:25 NASB

My teenage daughter, Cassie, was killed for her faith at Columbine High School in Littleton, Colorado, on April 20, 1999. I wrote a book, *She Said Yes,* describing Cassie's life, how she came to faith, and how she said "yes" to her faith in the end. In my book, I quote a lot of Cassie's friends. Jordan, one friend, recalled Cassie sharing her priorities in the days preceding the Columbine shootings:

"Three or four weeks before the Columbine incident, I drove her [Cassie] to a birthday party, and there were about five of us girls standing around, talking about weight and looks, and Cassie said she was so tired of talking about such petty things. She said she was done with it—it did nothing for anybody except make them unhappy about how they appeared. She wanted us to stop thinking about ourselves, and be there for each other and for the important things in life."

The important things in Cassie's life became clear on April 20, 1999. It was Jesus all the way.

FIVE GOLDEN RINGS

June Hetzel,
education professor,
Biola University

There is an appointed time for everything.

ECCLESIASTES 3:1 NASB

Everyone admired Janice. She was cute, outgoing, and a cheerleader. I thought Janice had the perfect life—especially when I heard that her boyfriend gave her a promise ring during her sophomore year.

A few months later, though, I heard they broke up. However, in a few short weeks, Janice had another long-term relationship. Several months later, this fellow also gave her a ring.

By our junior year, Janice was on her third boyfriend. This time it was an engagement ring. All went well until several months later, they broke up.

Long story short, by the time Janice was nineteen, she had promised to marry five different guys, accepted rings from all of them, broken up with all of them, and kept every ring. What I didn't know at the time was that this long trail of broken relationships also included sex outside of marriage and some abortions.

Life is not always what it seems. Janice's life seemed exciting but ended in heartache. Other girls, who didn't date much or went slower with their relationships, often made wiser choices and had happier marriages. Prince Charming is worth the wait. Don't be deceived by the glitter of a golden ring.

MY FIRST-PLACE WINNER

Angela Risley,
student,
Oklahoma Christian University

He is before all things, and in Him all things hold together.
COLOSSIANS 1:17 NASB

'll never forget my first broken heart. As most teenage girls experience at one point or another, I had a huge crush in high school. This wasn't just any crush though. I was sure we would end up together someday, even if he didn't know it yet.

As time went on, I realized I was trying to be someone else instead of being me. I've always been outgoing, but when he was around, I craved his attention. As usual, the minute I forgot what my true focus should be, things started to fall apart. I found out a couple of weeks later that he was dating another girl. I was devastated. With her typical wisdom, my mom told me something I still haven't forgotten—"You must always be an 'I' before you can be a 'we.'"

I knew then that compromising my standards was not getting me any closer to becoming the best version of me—someone who puts God before everything else in life. Through my disappointment, I learned that I had something better than a boyfriend. I had complete trust in the only person who would never let me down—God, my first-place winner.

A SECURE HIDING PLACE

Brittany Waggoner,
college student and writer

> *You are my hiding place;*
> *you will protect me from trouble*
> *and surround me with songs of deliverance.*
>
> PSALM 32:7 NIV

In high school I did a lot of baby-sitting to earn extra cash. One of the little girls I baby-sat was a very compassionate little girl named Sophia. What I remember most about Sophia was her habit of rescuing every bug that managed to get into the house. Whenever she spotted one, she wanted me to catch it in a jar and release it outside. I once thought that she was playing in another room when I tried to kill a spider. She wasn't. Sophia came sprinting to my side, begging for the life of that spider. After I got the nasty little thing into a jar, she took it from me and gently carried it to the front lawn. She didn't even force it out of the jar. She waited patiently until the spider was ready to brave the jungle of the lawn.

This is a picture of what God does for us in stressful times. If we allow Him, God will surround us with His loving hands and give us a hiding place until we are strong enough to face the world again.

DEATH BLOW

Debbie Graham,
writer

"Never will I leave you; never will I forsake you."
HEBREWS 13:5 NIV

It was a day like any other day when it happened. Mom and Dad asked my sister and me to sit down at the table. Mom said Dad wouldn't be living with us anymore because she and Dad were getting a divorce! We asked where Dad was going to live. Dad said he would be staying at Grandma's house. Mom and Dad said they were fighting too much, and it wasn't good for them to stay together. Good for them? What about us?

Dad left home about a week later. I will never forget him walking out of the house with the last of his things in a paper grocery bag. Dad gave me one of his policemen's patches as a memento and said he would see the two of us next weekend. Death came to our family that day. Life for me from then on was sad, unstable, frustrating, and frightening.

In those dark days, I thought I was alone. Now, as I look back over those years, I see a faithful friend who was with me and never left me. His love has brought me to a place of peace and plenty. His name is Jesus!

You Are God's Workmanship

Betsy Barber,
professor and psychologist,
with Michelle Lee

For we are God's workmanship,
created in Christ Jesus to do good works,
which God prepared in advance for us to do.
EPHESIANS 2:10 NIV

What are some of the things that you like to do the most or are good at doing? Are you interested in planes or reading? Are you good at singing or computers? What are some of your particular character traits? Maybe you are a thoughtful friend or a diligent worker. Have you ever thought about how God might use these interests, talents, and character traits to further His kingdom?

When I was growing up, I was smart and very social. I would spend hours talking to my friends! Now, as a professor and psychologist, I see how God has used both of these characteristics in my life. I get to spend my whole day being smart and talking with people! God had something for my life that fit with the way that He made me.

Did you know that you were also made for something? God has created you to do some specific good work. You are a part of the body of Christ (1 Corinthians 12), so consider what "part" God has created you to be, and remember that, in the body, every part is needed!

TRUE DELIGHT

Sheila Walsh,
writer and recording artist

*I will walk about in freedom,
for I have sought out your precepts.*
PSALM 119:45 NIV

There is liberty in knowing the Word of God and walking freely in its truths. Psalm 1 describes the pure happiness that comes from this intentional way of living: "But his delight is in the law of the LORD, and on his law he meditates day and night. He is like a tree planted by streams of water, which yields its fruit in season and whose leaf does not wither" (vv. 2–3 NIV).

Living with a clear conscience and a light heart has nothing to do with our own rules or judgments or small, confined perspectives. Rather, the key to personal liberty is delighting in God's Word. In *Mere Christianity,* C. S. Lewis writes, "To become holy is rather like joining a secret society. To put it at the very lowest, it must be great fun."

What a wonderful perspective! We make our lives so much more complicated than they need to be. We wonder where the narrow road is. We wonder if the person to our right or left is "doing it right." We wonder if anyone is noticing how hard we are trying.

God says, "Focus on Me! Love Me, delight in My ways, and be free!"

DON'T LET THE SUN GO DOWN

Jennifer Knapp,
recording artist

> *"In your anger do not sin": Do not let the sun*
> *go down while you are still angry,*
> *and do not give the devil a foothold.*
>
> EPHESIANS 4:26–27 NIV

Isn't it crazy? Sometimes the very people you love the most are the same people you get angry with the most! I guess this isn't a surprise to God—as He inspired people to write the Scriptures, He made provisions for the anger that we all deal with from time to time. God gave us basic principles to help us deal with anger, and when we violate them, we pay a price.

So, you say, how do I deal with it? Well, anger is definitely a complex problem, but here's an approach I use for handling tough situations. There is a phrase I like that goes like this: "Thoughts disentangle themselves when they pass over lips and fingertips." I suggest that first you practice talking to Jesus; second, talk to a Christlike friend; third, write it down; and finally, give it back to Jesus. This part of life is hard, but it's worth it to develop a habit of dealing with anger in the right way.

By the way, don't ever just go to sleep on it. Trust me—it doesn't work.

SILENCE AND SOLITUDE ARE
A FRAME OF MIND

Deirdre Cantrell,
director of new believers ministry,
Saddleback Church

"Be still, and know that I am God."

PSALM 46:10 NIV

We live in a society where we seldom experience true silence. Even when we turn off the television or unplug the phone, we still can hear the humming of the refrigerator or a chirping bird outside. Additionally, in living with our families or being with others at work, finding solitude can be a real challenge. However, does this have to mean we can't experience some type of silence and solitude before the Lord? Are we doomed to only wait until that perfect moment when we are alone with our Bibles for reading and prayer?

Several times throughout my day, I take what some call "minute retreats." I like to call them "heavenly havens." Have you taken a heavenly haven lately? This is where you consciously turn your mind for a few moments in silence and solitude before the Lord. All you do is take a few minutes to come into the presence of God.

The next time you're waiting for a friend or waiting in line, take a "heavenly haven." Be still before the Lord and know that He is God.

BEAUTY IS SOUL DEEP

MY STRENGTH AND SONG

June Hetzel,
education professor,
Biola University

The Lord is my strength and song,
and he is become my salvation.

EXODUS 15:2 KJV

Growing up, things weren't perfect. For example, my uncle was an alcoholic. Every time he came to visit, he had a bottle in a brown paper sack. I loved my uncle, and I could put up with his loud talking and wild humor, but one thing I didn't like was when I rode in his car. He always drove well over the speed limit. Even as a kid, I knew it wasn't safe—even though it was fun to zoom around.

But then the sobering event came. My best friend, Helen, was killed in a car accident. The accident occurred because a drunk driver sped down the freeway, just like my uncle. He lost control of his car, hitting Helen's car head on. She died instantly. My uncle didn't kill Helen, but it was a man who was like my uncle. From that day forward, I knew I would never get in a car with a drunk driver—no matter who they were. Neither would I allow a substance, like alcohol or drugs, to control my life. The Lord would be "my strength and my song," and I would not look to substance abuse for a momentary joy ride.

MY SISTER, MY FRIEND

Carla Perez,
teacher, mother, sister, friend

A friend loves at all times,
And a brother (sister) is born for adversity.
PROVERBS 17:17 NASB

Sure we were sisters, but sisters are sisters, and friends are friends. The party was with my friends. We had planned a whole night of "teenage" things. We were, after all, thirteen. What would we have in common with my twelve-year-old little sister? She pleaded and negotiated with our parents for a week, but I emerged victorious. I could go, and Donna would stay.

As I packed, Donna grew increasingly quiet. No arguments, no door slamming—just quiet (totally out of character for her). As I left for the party, Donna waved, her eyes glistening with unshed tears, her chin trembling slightly behind her smile. Then I recognized something I had not seen in my sister before—courage. I suddenly knew what my victory had cost her.

I wish that right then I had said, "Okay, go pack. You can come." I didn't. That would have been admitting my own selfishness. I wasn't willing to do that.

After the party, however, our relationship changed. I apologized; she forgave me. That night we became more than sisters, we became friends.

STAND TALL

Beverly Plaugher,
writer

For as he thinks within himself, so he is.
PROVERBS 23:7 NASB

My father said, "Stand tall, walk tall, and think tall."
I do not think he meant height only. You can
stand tall by the way you think, act, treat others, and the
way you treat yourself.

Keeping your skin shiny, nails filed, hair clean,
teeth brushed, breath fresh, your body well rested so
your eyes sparkle, and showering every day. . .these
habits of good hygiene say a lot about you as a young
woman. But, even more than excellent grooming habits,
there is the most precious habit of keeping your mind
and thoughts well groomed and clean.

So many television shows, movies, commercials,
lyrics, and magazines contaminate our minds with
unclean thoughts. As the old saying goes, "Garbage in,
garbage out." Wrongful living begins in the thought
life—right living begins in the thought life. Fill your
mind with pure thoughts—Scripture, truth, worship
music, and great books.

My dad was right. "Stand tall, walk tall, think
tall." It all begins in the thought life. Be wary of what
you allow to enter your thoughts for "as she thinks
within herself, so she is" (Proverbs 23:7 paraphrased).

ASHLEY'S AUDITIONS

Ashley, high school student, Gahanna, Ohio
Written by Krishana Kraft of *Brio*

"We must obey God rather than men."

ACTS 5:29 NASB

I'm very involved in theater, so when the director of theater productions at my high school asked me if I was auditioning for the fall play, I was really excited. She never asks people if they're auditioning, so that meant I probably had a good shot at a part. I went and read the script. But as I was reading, I realized there was no way I could be involved in this production because it was filled with derogatory remarks and cussing.

Why did I want to do this if I couldn't bring my little sisters to the show? I decided that if I wouldn't want God to be in the audience, then I shouldn't audition.

I went back to the director and told her how I felt. She said, "Okay," and left it at that. I thought I'd ruined my chances of ever having a part in a high school production. But God works in amazing ways, and that was not the case. Since then, I've had a leading role in a spring musical and made an advanced theater class, which also requires an audition.

Many people thought I was crazy for telling her what I did, but in the end I think it made a difference. I gained a lot of respect for that and discovered that since that incident, the director has cut down the bad language in the productions she has chosen.

TRAPPED IN A LIE

Deborah McIntire,
educator and author

> *The deeds of a man's hands will return to him.*
> PROVERBS 12:14 NASB

When I was in high school, three friends and I decided to see what it was like to skip school. We had never done anything like this before, but the idea intrigued us. We agreed a day shopping would be just the ticket. Since none of us could drive, we would take the bus. However, the bus never came, so we headed to my house. Once there, I called the bus line only to find out that the bus drivers were on strike. There went our fun day at the mall.

We decided to salvage the day the best we could. Unfortunately, before we could formulate a plan, we heard my dad unexpectedly arrive home. "Quick," I whispered. "He can't find us here. Hide in my closet. He probably won't stay long." Unfortunately, he did stay long, and the closet grew smaller by the minute—my girlfriends were furious.

Two hours later, after lunch and several work-related calls, my father finally left. Not only had we not gone shopping, the four of us had spent the entire afternoon crowded in a small, narrow closet, trapped in a lie. It was a lesson learned the hard way.

WARDROBE CHECK

Barbara Johnson,
Women of Faith speaker

"And so, as those who have been chosen of God,
holy and beloved, put on a heart of compassion, kindness,
humility, gentleness, and patience."

COLOSSIANS 3:12 NASB

Like everybody else, I have to get up and get dressed every day. Too often I go to my closet and throw my hands in the air: "I don't have anything to wear!"

"This jacket is too worn," I say to myself. "That blouse hangs wrong at the shoulders; why did I let my sister talk me into buying it? This little number is totally outdated; I can't wear that. This skirt is too long. This one's too short."

I sit on the edge of my bed and pout: "Nothing to wear!"

Seasons come and go. Clothing styles change. . . good thing I have another closet with unlimited choices. I have a wardrobe that will never fade, wear out, or go out of style. Best of all, these clothes fit perfectly each time I pull them out and put them on.

Have you checked your spiritual wardrobe lately?

Put away the shabby clothing of the past and enjoy all the garments in your spiritual wardrobe. . . kindness, gentleness, patience. . .dress like the young woman God made you to be!

FLY BOYS

Mary Crist,
dean of school of education,
California Baptist University

> *"Pride goes before destruction,*
> *and a haughty spirit before stumbling."*
> PROVERBS 16:18 NASB

I had good friends in high school, but "popular" guys never asked me out. However, we lived near an air force base, and I did occasionally date "fly boys."

One time a young officer invited me to go flying with him. What an exciting date, certainly better than any school event! After I had bragged to everyone, the unthinkable happened. My date stood me up without even a phone call. I was devastated.

To face people at school, I had to admit my arrogance. Real friends comforted me, and others ignored me. The result of trying to impress yielded little fruit. It was a painful lesson to learn, but I understand God's grace today because of it.

BE AN ENCOURAGER

Kelly Carr,
editor of *Encounter* Magazine

Pleasant words are a honeycomb,
sweet to the soul and healing to the bones.
PROVERBS 16:24 NIV

Think about a time when you were encouraged by someone. What did the person say? How did it make you feel? I've gotten encouragement notes that I've kept for years. People's kind words motivate me to keep going, keep trying, and keep giving life my all.

Am I doing the same for others? I don't hesitate to tell people that I like an outfit they're wearing or I like their new hairstyle. But how often do I compliment people on their great attitude or their godly character?

We find some good advice in Hebrews 10:24 (NLT): "Think of ways to encourage one another to outbursts of love and good deeds."

That's my challenge to you. Find ways to encourage people in their faith. Challenge them to stay strong, stick with Jesus, and keep living for Him.

Pick one person today to encourage. Tomorrow, pick someone else. Keep it up. Your encouragement can do as Scripture says and cause people to burst with love and good deeds!

ONE COURAGEOUS TEEN

Debra White Smith,
writer

Don't let anyone look down on you because you are young,
but set an example for the believers in speech,
in life, in love, in faith and in purity.

1 TIMOTHY 4:12 NIV

Joan of Arc was thirteen years old when she suspected that God was calling her to go to battle for her nation, France. The year was 1425, and the Hundred Years War was on between France and England.

By 1429, Joan was seventeen, and the English were about to capture the French city of Orléans. Believing that the Lord was asking her to help, Joan convinced Charles VII that she had a God-ordained mission to save her nation.

Joan led the French troops into battle and defeated the English. A little later, Charles VII was crowned king of France. At the coronation ceremony, Joan stood nearby in a place of honor. All this when she was only seventeen!

In 1430, when she was eighteen, Joan led another military operation against the English near Paris. She was then captured and sold to the English—who tried her, decided she was a heretic, and finally burned her at the stake on May 30, 1431, at the age of nineteen.

Eventually, she was formally named a saint. For centuries both men and women have admired her bravery and willingness to run headlong into battle on a divine mission.

ENDURANCE

Brittany Waggoner,
college student and writer

*Endure hardship with us like a
good soldier of Christ Jesus.*
2 TIMOTHY 2:3 NIV

Last fall, I decided to go running with my roommate, Rachel. I knew that she was an athlete but figured that I could keep up. Little did I know that Rachel had been on the track team in high school and had been running three miles every day during the summer. Needless to say, I couldn't keep up with her. Why? Because I did not have the endurance that she had.

Endurance is not only important to our physical bodies; enduring hard times in life is the key to developing spiritual maturity. God does not want us to remain baby Christians forever. There are many Christians who don't want to grow up spiritually, but we need to grow up. God wants us to mature into adult Christians who take on more responsibility in His kingdom.

Spiritual maturity should be our goal, and we should be willing to endure whatever it takes to achieve it.

GNATS AND GRACE

Martha Bolton,
writer

*"If any one of you is without sin,
let him be the first to throw a stone at her."*
JOHN 8:7 NIV

Do you overlook your own faults while putting other people's faults under a microscope? It's easy to do. Jesus even talked about this kind of human behavior when He said to the Pharisees, "You strain out a gnat, but swallow a camel." In other words, they were fretting over everyone else's minor infractions of the law, while ignoring their own major ones.

Jesus said something similar to His disciples and the people gathered to hear Him speak one day. He said, "First take the plank out of your eye, and then you will see clearly to remove the speck from your brother's eye." Again, loosely translated it means, "Clean up that pile of debris you've shoved under your own bed before you criticize the pencil that rolled under your brother's or sister's."

When it comes to other people's faults, we must look at them as we would want Christ to look at our faults—through the eyes of grace.

TIME WITH GOD

Andrea Taylor,
journalist,
2003 Brio Girl for
Focus on the Family

Because Thy lovingkindness is better than life,
my lips shall praise thee.

PSALM 63:3 KJV

I's so important for me to spend time alone with Jesus every day. He loves me so much. I mean, He's even willing to talk with me when I'm wearing my blue flannel pajama pants and my gray sweatshirt that doesn't match, when my hair's a mess and my breath is. . .well. . .not good. He meets me in His golden splendor just to remind me that He loves me, and He wants to take care of all the day will hold.

When I get up, and I'm still a little sleepy, I picture Him wide-awake watching me. I grab my Bible, and I make my first thoughts and actions all about Him. I lay down the day and let Him take control. It isn't always easy to get up early. Sometimes the warm covers call my name a little too loudly, but I know that Jesus' love is better than life or sleep (Psalm 63:3)! So when the world outside is cold and dark, I get up and let the light and love of the Father, my Best Friend, invade me.

BEAUTY IS SOUL DEEP

BUT NO ONE ASKED ME

La Verne Tolbert, Ph.D.,
psychologist and author

> *"I the LORD do not change."*
> MALACHI 3:6 NIV

Divorce. The words shook her like an earthquake. "But no one asked me!" Michelle ran out of the house and didn't stop running until she reached the church. She sat on the steps sobbing and begging God to please do something.

Mrs. Austin, the church's florist, drove up. "Are you all right?" she asked. "What a silly question. Of course you're not all right. What on earth has happened to you, child?"

As Michelle answered, years of frustration came tumbling out. It was an hour later that she finished telling about her parents' arguments and pending divorce. Now, divorce would change everything. But no one asked permission to ruin her life. She felt so alone.

Finally, Mrs. Austin spoke. "Even though your life is changing, like these flowers, you'll continue to bloom through the pain. God is with you, child. Jesus will never leave you or forsake you."

I wish there was a happier ending to the story, but there isn't. Michelle's parents did divorce, and her life changed in many ways. But Michelle knew that she had a friend in Jesus and that He would never, never leave her. Everything else might change, but He remained the same.

WHO WILL I MARRY?

Jeanetta Sims,
instructor,
Oklahoma Christian University

Has not the LORD made them one?
In flesh and spirit they are his.
And why one? Because he was
seeking godly offspring.

MALACHI 2:15 NIV

When I was in high school, I wondered who I would marry. "What will he look like? Where will he be from? Do I currently know him?" Of course, tops on my list of husband criteria was for him to be handsome, tall, and with an athletic build. It was a given that he would be a Christian.

At the advice of a missionary's wife, I later wrote every attribute I wanted in a husband and began to pray to God for a man with all of these attributes. My lengthy list ranged from as serious as being God-fearing, grounded in God's Word, and faithful in Christian stewardship to as fun-filled as loving to sing, taking me to McDonald's, and massaging my feet. I was faithful in dating only the boys who met the attributes on my list.

Years later I discovered that while I was praying for the man of my list, my husband was praying for a woman that met his criteria. I don't know who you will marry, but I am confident God's desire is for you to have a godly marriage. He can bless you with a godly man. So develop your list, start praying, and remain faithful.

STOP COMPARING

Luci Swindoll,
Women of Faith speaker and author

For we are not bold to class or compare ourselves
with some of those who commend themselves;
but when they measure themselves by themselves and compare
themselves with themselves, they are without understanding.

2 CORINTHIANS 10:12 NASB

When Scripture teaches that it is not wise to measure or compare ourselves with others, I think we should pay attention. When we compare, we almost always come up short. Or, perhaps worse, we decide we're better than someone else. Either way, it causes stress.

If you're not happy with who you are, you'll spend precious energy trying to be somebody you're not, and it will wear you out. Think for a moment. Is there anybody in your life you're comparing yourself to? A beautiful sister? An accomplished brother? A friend who never seems to have problems? A sports figure who excels with little effort? Well, may I say with all the love in the world: Quit it. That business of comparing is going to make you sick and unproductive, if it hasn't already. You are you. God made you, you. And you are exactly who He wants you to be. Don't be somebody's clone. That person you're trying to be may very well be trying to be you.

Let's just all relax and be ourselves. It's so much easier. And a lot more fun.

BEAUTY IN THE EYE
OF THE BEHOLDER

June Hetzel,
education professor,
Biola University

I will give thanks to You,
for I am fearfully and wonderfully made.
PSALM 139:14 NASB

When I was a teenager, I felt self-conscious about my looks. I wore thick glasses and braces. I was so self-conscious about getting food in my braces that I hardly ate at school during my teen years. Along with the glasses and braces, my parents would not allow me to wear makeup until I was eighteen. And, my dad would not let me get my ears pierced, claiming it was a "pagan" custom!

When I became eighteen, I was finally done with braces, glasses, and naked ear lobes. I now had a non-metallic smile, contacts, pierced ears, and makeup. But the funny thing was that all of the outer stuff really didn't change how I felt about myself inside. I still felt self-conscious, especially around the opposite sex. Suddenly I realized it was all in my head. It was the way I viewed myself. I needed to love me the way God made me. I needed to become comfortable with myself. I needed to stop comparing myself with the popular girls and see myself as God's beautiful creation.

JUST TO ABIDE

Gigi Graham Tchividjian,
writer and daughter of Billy Graham

"Remain in me, and I will remain in you.
No branch can bear fruit by itself; it must remain in the vine.
Neither can you bear fruit unless you remain in me."

JOHN 15:4 NIV

I prayed fervently, O Lord, please let this be the day you and I get it together!

After reading a portion of my Bible, I prayed again, giving the Lord my day. I felt so good. It was all so beautiful. Surely I wouldn't blow it today.

I tried. I really did. But my spirituality didn't even make it all the way through breakfast. First I argued with one of my sisters, then I talked back to my mother when she scolded me. Then, when I realized what I had done, I became so discouraged, I just gave up on that day completely.

So goes the story of my life. Trying so hard. . .and falling so short. I am a struggler. I'm always wishing I could eliminate this or that problem of weakness. Living the Christlike life just hasn't come easily for me.

One part of becoming truly spiritual is to abide, to focus on belonging to Him, and He will take care of the rest. As Corrie ten Boom used to say, "We need to quit struggling and start snuggling."

LOVE ONE ANOTHER

Mother Teresa,
Nobel Peace Prize winner

"Love one another.
As I have loved you,
so you must love one another."
JOHN 13:34 NIV

The greatest disease in the West today is not TB or leprosy; it is being unwanted, unloved, and uncared for. We can cure physical diseases with medicine, but the only cure for loneliness, despair, and hopelessness is love. There are many in the world who are dying for a piece of bread, but there are many more dying for a little love. The poverty in the West is a different kind of poverty—it is not only a poverty of loneliness but also of spirituality. There's a hunger for love, as there is a hunger for God.

When you know how much God is in love with you, then you can only live your life radiating that love. I always say that love starts at home: family first and then your own town or city. It is easy to love people who are far away, but it is not always so easy to love those who live with us or right next to us. I do not agree with the big way of doing things—love needs to start with an individual. To get to love a person, you must contact that person, become close. Everyone needs love. All must know that they're wanted and that they are important to God.

GOD'S TIMING

Kathy Troccoli,
recording artist and writer

> *I wait for the LORD, my soul waits,*
> *and in his word I put my hope.*
> PSALM 130:5 NIV

I want to do. I want to say. I want to act. I'm so guilty of getting in the way of God's timing. To learn to wait has been so difficult for me. I want to "fix" things quickly: the comment someone said about me; the comment I said about someone; the sudden news that turns my whole world upside down; the misunderstanding; the wanting to prove my point or the validity of my character; the uncomfortable changes life often brings.

I would like God to involve Himself in my circumstance according to my timing and my agenda. I forget how holy and perfect His ways, His timing, and His agenda are. Yet, over and over, I see that when I wait, letting Him be God, then He is God.

The circumstances of life can embitter any of us at any time. But if we allow it, God's grace and love can empower us and help us move through these times victoriously. As Oswald Chambers says, "It is not our circumstance, but God in our circumstance."

WHAT MATTERS MOST

Martha Bolton,
writer

*"But seek first his kingdom and his righteousness,
and all these things will be given to you as well."*

MATTHEW 6:33 NIV

God doesn't care about the size of your savings account, but He is interested in how much good you do with what you have.

God doesn't care whether or not you're wearing the hottest new shoes, but He does care where you walk in them.

The size of your house doesn't matter to God, but the size of your heart does.

Your grade point average, the college you get accepted into, or even your major doesn't impress God as much as how you treat others.

Your popularity doesn't matter to God, but He is interested in whether you've told your friends about Him.

How well you're connected doesn't matter as much to God as how well you're grounded.

God doesn't care if you can quote the law, but He is concerned with how much mercy you show others.

The frequency with which you go to church doesn't matter as much to God as the openness of your heart while you're there.

The size of your offering doesn't impress Him as much as how much of yourself accompanies it.

God isn't as concerned with how boldly you speak for Him as He is with how boldly you live for Him.

NO ROOM FOR LUKEWARM CHRISTIANS

Misty Bernall,
mother of teen martyr Cassie Bernall

> " 'He who overcomes will thus be clothed in white garments;
> and I will not erase his name from the book of life, and I will
> confess his name before My Father, and before His angels.' "

REVELATION 3:5 NASB

Living as a Christian is filled with challenges. A friend of my daughter's wrote to Cassie before the high school shooting that took my daughter's life. In the letter, Cassie's friend described her struggles in her Christian walk:

Dear Cass,

. . .I know I need to give it all to Christ, but it's so hard. Just when I think I'm getting the hang of giving it all up, I find myself trying to take control of my life. . . . If I could only let my pride fall, I might be able to finally find a sense of peace and let down the barrier that is keeping me from growing in God.

I need to be completely honest with myself and to God and stop thinking I can fool him—He's God, for crying out loud! And I can't make compromises. It's like being lukewarm—He'll spit me out if I keep it up. I can't ride the fence one day, trying to convince myself I'm just "reaching out to people" by acting "normal" and then trying to be a dedicated Christian the next.

There is no room for lukewarm Christians. This is life. Play it straight.

GIVE HIM PRAISE

Shirley Dobson,
wife of Dr. James Dobson,
founder of Focus on the Family

Through Him then, let us continually
offer up a sacrifice of praise to God,
that is, the fruit of lips that give thanks to His name.
HEBREWS 13:15 NASB

O n a beautiful Saturday afternoon, we entered the
Los Angeles Memorial Coliseum and settled into
our seats. . . . At one end of the field, a huge mass of
players. . .huddled together. The crowd buzzed expec-
tantly. Suddenly, the players raced en masse toward the
center of the field as the band burst into the USC fight
song. The crowd. . .rose as one and delivered a thunder-
ous ovation for the young heroes. Fans clapped, raised
their arms, and voiced their admiration. . . .

For thousands of us, the exhilaration we felt was
total and genuine. But a question [remained]: If we
can respond like this to a group of college student athletes, how much more awe and enthusiasm should we
be willing to show to our heavenly Father?

In any discussion of this nature, it's important to
remember that God is not our "genie in a bottle"—He
is not simply waiting in heaven to receive our laundry
list of. . .requests. On the contrary, God is worthy of
our praise and pleased when we come before Him
with thanksgiving. He wants to be appreciated, just as
we do.

BEAUTY IS SOUL DEEP

FACE YOUR FEAR

Nancy C. Anderson,
actress and playwright

> *Whenever I am afraid, I will trust in You.*
> PSALM 56:3 NKJV

When I was in tenth grade, I was painfully shy. I would usually walk through the hall with my head down and my arms tightly crossed. So, I amazed myself when I decided to try out for the school play.

I loved the musical *Oklahoma* and had a secret dream to be on stage. So I faced my fear of rejection and prayed for the Lord to give me strength and a strong voice as I auditioned.

I was thrilled when they gave me the part of Townswoman #3. The rehearsals were a lot of fun, and I made many new friends. It was great to discover the wonderful feeling of being part of a group with a common goal.

My shyness and fear almost kept me from that experience. But, since I took the steps to go beyond my comfort zone, the Lord has used me to write and perform in thirty-five drama productions for Christian theater. Don't let fear hold you back from the things that God has called you to do.

VALENTINE'S DAY BLUES

Natalie Lloyd,
author and *Brio* columnist

Man's steps are ordained by the Lord.
PROVERBS 20:24 NASB

It's inevitable. This is the time of the year we sit down in front of the VCR, pop in *Anne of Green Gables*, and scream, "Where is my Gilbert?!" as popcorn spews from our mouths like confetti. I start to think about "him" and wonder where he is or if I've met him or if maybe I overlooked him.

I get confused about "friendships" that look a lot like dating and wonder when or if they're ever suddenly going to turn into something else. We're created to love and be loved, and sometimes that seems just a little too confusing to me! It takes a lot of effort to put all of that in the hands of God and say, "I trust You. This is Yours." Yet in that process over the years, He's taught me some cool things. I hope you'll trust Him along the way too and be patient for His blessing.

BEAUTY IS SOUL DEEP

53

ANCHOR IN THE STORM

Lisa Beamer,
wife of September 11 hero Todd Beamer

*"As for you, you meant evil against me,
but God meant it for good in order
to bring about this present result,
to preserve many people alive."*

GENESIS 50:20 NASB

The mention of September 11 brings to mind floods of memories and emotions for all of us. For most Americans, feelings of sadness, disbelief, anger, and frustration prevail. Added to these for my family is the incredible personal pain of the loss of Todd, our husband, father, son, and brother. With only these human emotions to draw upon, I'm afraid I wouldn't be able to even breathe at times.

The good news (yes, there's good news!) is that God is faithful each moment to provide the supernatural resources I need not only to carry on, but to be even joyful on occasion. . . .

. . .Truly we have lost much, but we have gained much as well. As Joseph said to his brothers in Genesis 50:20 (NIV), I say to the originators of the evil acts of September 11: " 'You intended to harm me, but God intended it for good to accomplish what is now being done, the saving of many lives.' "

. . .Although I suffer indescribable human pain, the knowledge of God's eternal good coming from these events is an unwavering anchor for me.

TUNING IN TO GOD

Joy Mosbarger,
college professor

My soul waits in silence for God only;
From Him is my salvation.
He only is my rock and my salvation,
My stronghold; I shall not be greatly shaken.

PSALM 62:1–2 NASB

Sometimes my world seems to be filled with unending noise. Some of it is external noise—televisions blaring, boom boxes blasting, phones ringing, garbage trucks beeping, people yelling. Some of it is internal noise—voices in my mind reminding me of all the things I have to do, places I have to go, people I have to see. And all this noise makes it hard to hear the voice of God. Yet I long to hear His voice, to get His advice, to sense His encouragement, to know He loves me.

I know that to discern His voice, I need to get away to a quiet place and wait for the external and internal noise to still. That can take awhile, and I often get restless and squirmy. But if I continue to wait patiently, I always find that it's worth it, because only in that place of silent listening do I find the nourishment, instruction, and hope that I need. I can continue on in peace and confidence and strength in the midst of the noise. And then, no matter what happens, I will not be greatly shaken, because my rock and I are once again on the same wavelength.

BEAUTY IS SOUL DEEP

Love Creates Good

Elisabeth Elliot,
writer and missionary

Praise be to the God and Father of our Lord Jesus Christ,
the Father of compassion and the God of all comfort,
who comforts us in all our troubles,
so that we can comfort those in any trouble
with the comfort we ourselves have received from God.

2 Corinthians 1:3–4 niv

Love, it seems, creates good—by drawing good out of any situation through suffering. The suffering itself thereby becomes a pathway to holiness.

Out of suffering comes holiness—in these forms: comfort, consolation, the fellowship of Christ's suffering, salvation, strength, fortitude, endurance. This is what is meant by redemptive suffering. The greater the measure allotted to us, the greater is our material for sacrifice. As we make it a joyful offering to God, our potential is enhanced for becoming "instruments of His peace"—being "broken bread and poured-out wine," overflowing with consolation for the lonely and the suffering of the world.

Do we want to be servants to one another in love? Let God turn even our loneliness into power to serve. Let Him free us from ourselves in order that we may become the servants of others. As the basis of our union with Christ is His sacrificial love for us, so the basis of our union with others is that same sort of love—the love that forgets itself and its own troubles and lays itself down.

DRAWING NEAR
THROUGH TRIALS

Sheila Walsh,
writer and recording artist

We were under great pressure, far beyond our ability to endure,
so that we despaired even of life. Indeed, in our hearts we felt
the sentence of death. But this happened that we might not
rely on ourselves, but on God, who raises the dead.

2 CORINTHIANS 1:8-9 NIV

St. Patrick, the patron saint of Ireland, was born in Britain in the fourth century. He was raised in a religious home, but there is no historical indication that he had a relationship with Christ until he went through an unbelievable trial that transformed him.

When Patrick was sixteen years old, he was kidnapped by Irish pirates and held captive for eight years. He escaped when he was twenty-four and returned to his family a changed man. He came back with a passion for God, with a deep commitment to Christ, and a sense of divine calling on the rest of his life. He trained for ministry and spent himself in the cause of Christ. When he died at about seventy years of age, he left behind a moving account of his personal journey with God.

History bears witness to the countless ways in which even the harshest trials seem to carve God's initials on our souls and draw us close to His heart. I have talked to many people who acknowledge that they would never have chosen the path they found themselves on, but having walked that way, they would never change it now.

MY GUY

Debbie Graham,
writer

" 'Love the Lord your God with all your heart and
with all your soul and with all your mind.' "

MATTHEW 22:37 NIV

Let me tell you about my guy. He's tall, strong, honest, loyal, and most importantly, loves Jesus.

I love my guy and trust him implicitly. He's proven his character to me over and over again. However, for all the good that flows from his heart, he is still just a guy. Sometimes he's cranky, and sometimes he just doesn't tell me what he's feeling.

I have learned there is only one person who is worthy of the gift of my entire heart, only one person who is entirely trustworthy. There is only one person who is always thinking about what's best for me. This guy is Jesus. Jesus is always there to hear my deepest thoughts and to fill the holes in my heart. His name and His person are worthy of nothing short of owning my entire being. Jesus is the love of my life. By the way, He's also given me a great guy.

When Being "Nice" Means Not Being Nice!

Shelly Cunningham,
Christian education professor,
Biola University

My brothers, if one of you should wander from the truth
and someone should bring him back, remember this:
Whoever turns a sinner from the error of his way
will save him from death and cover over
a multitude of sins.

JAMES 5:19–20 NIV

Imagine that you and your friend are at the mall. At one of the shops, your friend tries on an outfit. She seems eager for your approval, but you know it's a mismatch. Neither the color nor the style fits her. Do you tell her the truth—save her money and embarrassment? Or, do you force a smile and tell her what she wants to hear?

Now imagine that there's more at risk than a mismatched outfit. What if a friend is making choices you know could wreck her life? Do you pretend not to notice?

The verses above challenge Christians to show true love and care by letting someone know when they are beginning to wander from doing the right thing. Sometimes the most incredible gift you can give to a friend is to tell her the truth, especially when no one else has the guts to do it.

WHAT A CONCEPT!

Martha Bolton,
writer

"Do to others as you would have them do to you."

LUKE 6:31 NIV

Do unto others as you would have them do unto you. We've heard that hundreds of times, haven't we? Yet what exactly does it mean?

It means:

If you don't like people talking about you behind your back, don't talk about other people behind their backs.

If you want to be forgiven for what you do wrong to others, forgive others for what they do wrong to you.

If you want to be included in others' social plans, include others in your social plans.

If you want your friends to listen to you, listen to them.

If you want people to be considerate of your feelings, be considerate of other people's feelings.

If you want people to overlook your faults, overlook other people's faults.

If you don't want people holding a grudge against you, don't hold a grudge against them.

It's a rather simple concept, but it's important enough that Jesus summed up all the "laws" with these two—"Love the Lord your God with all your heart and with all your soul, and with all your strength, and with all your mind," and "Love your neighbor as yourself."

So simple. So life-changing. And so often overlooked.

SACRIFICE

Rebecca St. James,
recording artist

*"And everyone who has left houses or brothers or sisters or father
or mother or children or fields for my sake will receive a hundred
times as much and will inherit eternal life."*

MATTHEW 19:29 NIV

A few years back, my dad went through a real humbling, growing time in his life. Through it he learned a lot about sacrifice. When we moved to the States, Dad had to leave his record company and business in Australia. Unfortunately, without him there, it fell apart. He had to let go of something he'd poured his soul into for fifteen years. One morning he was so down about it that he couldn't get out of bed. That same day, Eric Champion's father called and asked him to manage Eric. Through the pain of sacrifice, God had shown His power.

[Then] in August of 1993, my grandpa, who lived in Australia, was diagnosed with cancer. They operated on him, and he seemed to be getting better. But, then he came down with pneumonia, and because he was so weak, he died. It was an extremely hard time for my family because we were on the other side of the world and loved him so much. But it was hardest on my dad, who couldn't be there to say good-bye to his father. Because of this pain, it made us really see that there is a cost involved in following God's will.

GREEN PASTURES AND STILL WATERS

Lorraine Peterson,
writer

> *The LORD is my shepherd, I shall not be in want.*
> *He makes me lie down in green pastures,*
> *he leads me beside quiet waters, he restores my soul.*
>
> PSALM 23:1–3 NIV

Jesus promises to give us peace. Most of us think of peace as vacationing on a Caribbean island or being able to sleep until noon on Saturday morning. Yet if peace means escape, the only way to get it is to drop out of regular day-to-day living, with its overdue library books, traffic jams, and tight schedules. Fortunately Jesus offers peace that the world can't give—peace when your mother yells at you, peace when the car runs out of gas, and peace when the band bus leaves without you—peace in the middle of pressure.

An artist once portrayed "peace" as a little bird content in a nest on the end of an oak branch sticking out over roaring Niagara Falls. That is peace.

Paul commands us to "let the peace of Christ rule" in our hearts. If you keep your mind on Jesus and you look to Him in faith, you'll find green pastures and still waters, even in the middle of the fifth-hour English class and other unexpected places.

SUFFERING

Joni Eareckson Tada,
quadriplegic writer and speaker

"The LORD gave and the LORD has taken away.
Blessed be the name of the LORD."

JOB 1:21 NASB

In the aftermath of this terrible tragedy [September 11], people asked, "Why?" Many wondered at the goodness of God and the problem of so much evil and suffering. Their questions reflect ours as we face our own personal crisis. . . .

As Dr. Peter Kreeft suggested, "When a person is suffering, that person is like a little child looking up into the face of his daddy and asking, 'Why?' The child doesn't want answers or reasons why so much as to have Daddy pick him up and reassure him that everything is going to be okay."

Our heartfelt plea is for assurance—Fatherly assurance—that there is an order to reality that far transcends our problems. We need assurance that the world is not splitting apart at the seams, that it's not nightmarish chaos, that the world, our world, is orderly and stable, that somehow everything will be okay.

God must be the center of our suffering. What's more, He must be consummately good. He must be Daddy, personal, compassionate. This is our cry. And God, like a father, doesn't give advice—He gives Himself. . . .

LET YOUR WILL BE DONE

Charlotte Smith,
basketball player and Jones Cup Gold Medalist,
with Dave Branon

"Father, if You are willing, remove this cup from Me;
yet not My will, but Yours be done."

LUKE 22:42 NASB

[C]harlotte Smith's] mother had died. Where was God [in this]?

". . .The hardest thing was knowing what God was doing," Charlotte says now. "I didn't understand. For awhile, I was just angry with God."

"Why did You take my mom away?" I would ask [God]. "We needed her."

"That has been the hardest point in my walk with God," Charlotte says. "I. . .didn't want to open my Bible or pray or anything. I didn't think it was fair for Him to take my mom."

. . .The healing process for the young basketball star was gradual.

"I didn't really open up to anyone," Charlotte says. "I didn't think anyone knew how much I was struggling. . . ."

As the months wore on, though, Charlotte began to see her life return to a bit of normalcy. . . . "Time took away some of the pain, and I was able to accept it and move on."

[Charlotte] finally concluded, "Everything happens for a reason. I try not to question everything, but let God have His way. I just had to say, 'God, let Your will be done.' "

HOSPITALITY

Claire Sibold,
education professor

Be hospitable to one another.
1 PETER 4:9 NASB

Our neighbor Barbara Story was an amazing homemaker. Whenever I baby-sat her children, I saw evidence of her hard work and personal style. Her home was straight out of Better Homes and Gardens magazine; it was immaculate, yet cozy and inviting. Barbara always made me feel comfortable in her home. She often had freshly baked cookies on the counter and a hand-knit blanket on the couch so I could curl up in front of the television when Barbara and her husband were out late.

Barbara also had a beach cottage. I always felt welcome in her beach cottage too. Her special "touches" were everywhere. There were coordinated fabrics on the sofa and chairs, and once again a hand-knit blanket tossed over the back of the couch. Outside were clay pots containing strawberry plants, flowers, and herbs.

Because of Barbara's example of hospitality, I realized that even as a teenager, I could transform my bedroom into a beautiful and welcoming place. By adding fresh flowers from the garden, pictures of friends, or a hand-painted object to my room, it became a special place to study and "hang out" with my friends.

WHO ARE WE WORKING FOR?

Twila Paris,
recording artist

> *Whatever you do, work at it with all your heart,*
> *as working for the Lord, not for men, since you know that*
> *you will receive an inheritance from the Lord as a reward.*
> *It is the Lord Christ you are serving.*
>
> COLOSSIANS 3:23–24 NIV

When I was a teenager, I worked in my parents' Bible bookstore. Just the fact that it was my parents' store made me want to be sure I was always friendly, courteous, and helpful to everyone who came in. I was naturally aware that my attitude, demeanor, and performance would always reflect on my mom and dad.

If we, as Christians, would keep in mind who we are really working for, then we would consistently stand out as the most productive, efficient segment of society. Verse 23 says, "whatever you do"—meaning whether you are doing homework for your math teacher, cooking dinner for your family, building cars on an assembly line, or performing heart surgery—you are called to do it as unto the Lord. Our work then becomes a very practical form of worship.

God's rewards are based on faithfulness, not on how important we perceive our job to be. Let's purpose in our hearts that we will glorify God in our work today—whatever we do.

TWO ARE BETTER THAN ONE

Dyanna Espinoza,
art educator

But there is a friend who sticks closer than a brother.

PROVERBS 18:24 NASB

In my early teens, I went to parties where my friends drank and used drugs. When drugs were passed around, everyone said "yes," and it was harder and harder for me to say "no." One night my best friend Laurie and I talked about how we felt. Neither of us wanted to use drugs, but we were afraid we wouldn't be strong enough to keep saying "no." That night we made a pact to stick together—no matter what situation we were in, we could count on each other to make the right decision and say "no." Just knowing Laurie was there beside me gave me strength to keep doing the right thing.

A couple of years later, Laurie and I both became Christians, and I realized the Holy Spirit would continue to give me strength to make the right decisions for my life. I am so grateful I can count on God—and so thankful He gave me a special friend who was willing to stand beside me during those difficult times.

THE REAL ME?

Natalie Lloyd,
author and *Brio* columnist

There is no fear in love; but perfect love casts out fear.
1 JOHN 4:18 NASB

At this age, it's so easy to let dating determine our choices. But dating someone, no matter how cool he may be, will never make us feel complete. Only a personal relationship with Christ will do that. It's easy to get so caught up in a guy that we try to change everything—the way we act, the way we laugh, the way we talk. Suddenly, we may do (or not do) things we wouldn't have before. Even though I hate to admit it, I can think of several times I've put way too much thought into how I looked and acted just so a guy would take notice.

While it's no big deal to want to look good, and we need to be concerned with our actions, spending too much time on that can make us become very self-centered. And more often than I want to admit, I may act like someone I'm not. We don't have to change ourselves for someone who really loves us; he'll love us as we are. . .as Christ first loved us.

JESUS IN OUR THOUGHTS

Mother Teresa,
Nobel Peace Prize winner

Pray without ceasing.
1 THESSALONIANS 5:17 NASB

D oes your mind and your heart go to Jesus as soon as you get up in the morning? This is prayer, that you turn your mind and heart to God. In your times of difficulties, in sorrows, in sufferings, in temptations, and in all things, where did your mind and heart turn first of all? How did you pray? Did you take the trouble to turn to Jesus and pray, or did you seek consolations?

Has your faith grown? If you do not pray, your faith will [waver]. . . . Ask the Holy Spirit to pray in you. Learn to pray, love to pray, and pray often. Feel the need to pray and to want to pray.

If you have learned how to pray, then I am not afraid for you. If you know how to pray, then you will love prayer—and if you love to pray, then you will pray. Knowledge will lead you to love and love to service.

DO OPPOSITES REALLY ATTRACT?

Ramona Tucker and Jeff Tucker,
youth workers and authors

*Since we have gifts that differ according to the grace given to us,
each of us is to exercise them accordingly.*

ROMANS 12:6 NASB

Friendship isn't automatic. You don't just push a button on a machine and—*ka-chink*—out falls a perfect, made-to-order friend. Actually, that would be pretty boring. You don't need a duplicate copy of yourself as a friend—it would be like staring at yourself every day.

Friendship doesn't always mean agreeing. Differences can be good. They make us think and help us grow as individuals. . . .

Good friends learn to compromise and to give each other freedom to be who they are. They are dedicated to each other and to learning how to make their relationship work. Good friends let each other be unique, and they challenge each other to become the best they can be.

Some of the most unlikely people in the Bible were friends. Take Moses and Aaron, for example. Moses was a terrific organizer; God needed his talent when the Israelites were wandering in the desert. But Moses had a problem. He couldn't speak well—he'd get so nervous that he'd stutter and stumble over his words. He needed his brother, Aaron, who was a great speaker. . . . Together, Moses and Aaron were unstoppable.

FERTILIZER FOR A
BEAUTIFUL CHARACTER

Gigi Graham Tchividjian,
writer and daughter of Billy Graham

I want to know Christ and the power of his resurrection
and the fellowship of sharing in his sufferings,
becoming like him in his death, and so, somehow,
to attain to the resurrection from the dead.

PHILIPPIANS 3:10–11 NIV

Even if suffering is caused by the wrongdoing of others, so was our Lord's. Even if there is no explanation, we accept and worship and humbly acknowledge that a sovereign, loving God does not have to answer all of our questions or give a reason for all that He does or allows into our lives.

Someone once said, "Christ didn't come to take away all pain and suffering, nor did He come to explain it, but He came so that He might go through it with us."

Triumphant suffering is a wonderful fertilizer for a beautiful character. Some of the most beautiful Christians I know have suffered much.

If for some reason God has appointed you special trials, special burdens, special weights, rest assured that in His heart, He has also reserved a very special place for you.

Often the weight we carry is the anchor for our lives. It anchors us to the Lord Jesus. It keeps us dependent on Him and His strength.

WHAT A RUSH!

Kelly Carr,
editor of *Encounter* Magazine

*Peter said to him, "We have left all
we had to follow you!"*
LUKE 18:28 NIV

"There's a bunch of us going skydiving in a few weeks. Wanna come?"

I figured I was up for the challenge, so I said yes. A few people who were standing around looked at me like I was nuts.

When we went to skydive, we had to sign a release form to say that if we got hurt—or, worst-case scenario, if we happened to die—that we or our families would not sue.

I almost laughed out loud as I signed the paper. Yeah, I know that jumping out of a plane involves a slight risk.

To make a long story short, I jumped, it went well, and I had one of the biggest rushes of my life!

Being loyal to God can be risky too. For some people around the world, following Jesus can mean risking their lives.

Your risks may be different. You may risk your reputation, your friends, or your comfort zone. There are a number of things that you put on the line when you stick with Jesus.

But, when it's all said and done—what a rush!

THE BEAUTY OF GRACE

Joni Eareckson Tada,
quadriplegic writer and speaker

*But to each one of us grace has been given
as Christ apportioned it.*
EPHESIANS 4:7 NIV

Grace is what beauty looks like when it moves. God's grace is what He looks like when He moves, acting out His will through us.

Those on whom God's grace rests are truly. . .gracious. They are truly beautiful. The cerebral-palsied young man who smiles despite a dreary existence in a nursing home. The elderly woman who always seems to think of others rather than her aches and pains. The mother of two toddlers who is happy to baby-sit the neighbor's little boy. The pastor and his wife who take in a homeless couple for a week while they look for lodging. These people shine with a hint of glory. They shine because of God's grace.

Grace is God's energy, all bright, beautiful, and full of power. And grace is most beautiful when God is moving through us to touch the lives of others who hurt.

GOD IS BIGGER

Brittany Waggoner,
college student and writer

"I have swept away your offenses like a cloud,
your sins like the morning mist.
Return to me, for I have redeemed you."

ISAIAH 44:22 NIV

Becoming a Christian is like entering a maze, with numerous paths from which to choose. You live your life one way or another. You cannot take more than one path in the maze at once, nor can you live out your life both in obedience to God and according to your own selfish desires.

Sometimes you run into a dead end in life because you have made a bad decision. Because of where you have ended up, you feel a great amount of remorse for your decision. When this happens, you can decide whether to stay in the dead end, regretting the past, or turn around and search for the right passageway.

Sometimes we get stuck in a dead end because we cannot imagine God would forgive us of so great a sin. Drugs? Alcohol? Premarital sex? Betrayal of a friend? Cheating? Lying? Believe it or not, there is no mistake bigger than God's forgiveness. It is impossible for us to commit sins so great or so many that God will not take us back if we go to Him in true repentance, seeking to change our ways. This knowledge should not give us license to sin; it should spur us on to serve Him even more faithfully because of His mercy.

A SWEEPING VICTORY

Martha Bolton,
writer

*Therefore, get rid of all moral filth and the evil that is so prevalent
and humbly accept the word planted in you, which can save you.*
JAMES 1:21 NIV

D o you hate sweeping your floor? Sure, it's nice to
walk on after it's done, but the process can be a
pain, can't it? You might even be tempted to take a
shortcut and sweep all those dust balls, wads of paper,
broken pens, chewed-up pencils, paper clips, and whatever else has taken up residence on your floor under the
rug so no one will see them. But you know they're
there. God knows they're there. And your mom probably has a pretty good idea that they're there, too.

Sometimes we are tempted to take a few shortcuts
in cleaning up the messes in our lives too. Instead of
putting envy, jealousy, greed, lust, hatred, and pride
where they belong—under the grace of God—we try
to hang on to them and tuck them away in our hearts,
thinking no one will see them. We don't get rid of them;
we just hide them. But God knows they're still there.
And so do we.

Maybe it's time we all did a little spring-cleaning
in our hearts to see what we have hidden in there.

AMAZING GRACE!

Sheila Walsh,
writer and recording artist

O LORD, you have searched me and you know me.
You know when I sit and when I rise; you perceive my thoughts
from afar. You discern my going out and my lying down;
you are familiar with all my ways. Such knowledge is
too wonderful for me, too lofty for me to attain.

PSALM 139:1–3, 6 NIV

The legendary British prime minister, Sir Winston Churchill, was once asked, "Are you ready to meet your Maker?" He replied, "I am ready to meet my Maker. Whether He is ready for the ordeal of meeting me is another matter entirely."

But that is the wonder of the gospel. God knows us thoroughly and loves us completely. All human love is conditional. We hide from one another, believing (at times rightly so) that if we were fully known, we would not be accepted. But that is not true of our heavenly Father's love. He knows all our shadowed places and longs to fill them with His light.

The psalmist proclaims the wonder of the fact that God is familiar with all our ways. David was a man who knew shadows well. His choices resulted in the death of a man as he seduced the man's wife and arranged for him to be lost on the field of battle. Yet here he is able to sing praise to God. He does so not because he takes his sin lightly, but because he is confident that his God knows completely, loves totally, and forgives utterly.

MANAGING GOD'S STUFF

Joyce Miriam Brooks,
administrator,
Biola University

Wealth and honor come from you;
you are the ruler of all things.
In your hands are strength and power
to exalt and give strength to all. . . .
"Everything comes from you, and
we have given you only what comes from your hand."

1 CHRONICLES 29:12, 14 NIV

Do you own a CD player, a car, or a pair of jeans? If you think you do, think again. In God's eyes, you own nothing. Ultimately everything belongs to God. All that we have—our food, clothes, mind, energy, computer, money—everything we call ours comes from God. Not only that, but God holds us accountable for how we use them. We will have to give Him a report on what we did with His stuff.

So how are you using the things God has given you? Do you buy lots of cool outfits for yourself but forget to help clothe the poor? Do you spend money going to movies and neglect to give any to your church? Remember, you are the manager of God's stuff. What does He want you to do with it? Ask Him every day, starting today.

CANDY GOES TO CONGRESS

Kerry Stavert,
single parent of five

"Be strong and of good courage, do not fear."
DEUTERONOMY 31:6 NKJV

Everyone I knew in college loved Candy. She was pretty, smart, and full of energy. If you walked into a party and the only person you knew was Candy, you would have a great time. I was shocked to find out from a former high school friend of hers that this had not always been the case.

She explained, "No one even knew or noticed Candy our freshman year. Sometime during our sophomore year, Candy decided to change her withdrawn behavior. She started boldly approaching the most popular girls on campus and just started conversations with them. They treated her horribly, but she would just smile and ask them questions about themselves and tell them nice things. At first she was seen as a pest. Then people felt sorry for her. It wasn't long before they admired her courage and longed for some of her strength themselves. After awhile, Candy became a respected presence on campus."

I guess Candy's story shouldn't have surprised me. You see, the last I heard, Candy had this great job in Washington, D. C., working for members of Congress!

PRESS ON

Tina C. Elacqua, Ph.D.,
assistant professor,
Crichton College

*I press on toward the goal for the prize of the
heavenly call of God in Christ Jesus.*
PHILIPPIANS 3:14 NRSV

Have you ever felt like a failure? As I was growing up, I constantly felt like a failure. Every time I tried something, I failed. I took my driver's exam road test and failed. I tried out for the cheerleading squad and failed. I took the standardized test to qualify for advanced classes in algebra and failed.

However, the Spirit inside me did not let me give up. The Spirit told me that I could achieve all God had planned for my life. After taking a few more driving lessons, I took the driver's exam road test and passed. I tried out again for the cheerleading squad and made the team. I took the advanced algebra class on a trial basis and aced the exam!

The Lord has used these experiences to teach me about pressing on. The persistence and perseverance required to seek after the Lord's plan is worth the blessings that will follow. When we face failure, remember the Lord tells us that we can do all things through Christ who strengthens us (Philippians 4:13). I encourage you to believe in what God can do through you as you seek God's plan for your life. Press on!

LOST OPPORTUNITY

Deborah McIntire,
educator and writer

> *There is one who speaks rashly like the thrusts of a sword,*
> *But the tongue of the wise brings healing.*
>
> PROVERBS 12:18 NASB

David and I had been friends since kindergarten, and, to me, David's differences didn't matter. He stuttered and was slow when we played tag, but that was just sweet lovable David, who always greeted me with a shy, crooked smile.

By eighth grade, David's differences were the object of public ridicule. David now had acne and was overweight, the perfect target for snide remarks and cruel practical jokes. I was kind to David when we were alone and never joined the group ridicule; however, I never spoke out in defense of him because I was afraid that I would be ridiculed too.

David endured this cruelty for most of the school year. Then in early spring, he missed a week of school. I should have called, but didn't. By the time David missed a third week, I learned he was very ill and in the hospital. Cancer had permeated his body.

When I visited him, I wanted to say I was sorry, but I was too late. David was unconscious. A week later, he was dead. As I sat at David's funeral, I prayed, *Lord, from this day forward, help me to be a true friend regardless of the cost.*

SELF-IMAGE

Lorraine Peterson,
writer

*Whom have I in heaven but you? And earth has nothing I desire
besides you. My flesh and my heart may fail, but God is the
strength of my heart and my portion forever.*

PSALM 73:25–26 NIV

Do you ever feel worthless? Do zits, greasy hair, and a lack of poise get you down? Do you dwell on the fact that you are uncoordinated or a poor student or are not particularly popular?

Getting out of the low self-image syndrome involves deciding who is important to you and who is going to shape your image of yourself. If you let society do it, you will always come out a loser because no one can be good-looking, witty, successful, intelligent, athletic, musical, and well-informed, all at the same time. Every other TV commercial warns that you are lacking in some way.

If you decide that God is going to be so important in your life that nothing else matters, you'll sense God loving you and comforting you when no one else understands. The God who made the universe, controls the galaxies, and presides over history loves you—warts and all—with a constant love. In the light of this great fact, should what other people think of you be that important?

WHEN A CHILD COMES HOME

Sheila Walsh,
writer and recording artist

*"There is rejoicing in the presence of the angels of God
over one sinner who repents."*

LUKE 15:10 NIV

John Harper [was a] minister [who] went down with the Titanic. He was heading to America for an evangelistic crusade.

After [the ship] hit the giant iceberg, the captain cried, "Women and children first!" But one survivor claimed that John Harper cried, "Women, children, and the unsaved first!"

When the ship disappeared into the inky water, John found a piece of wood and held on. He saw a man float past him and, fighting for breath, asked, "Are you saved?" The man said no and floated off a ways. Then once more he passed John, and with his last breath, John Harper proclaimed, "Believe in the Lord Jesus Christ and you will be saved." Then the minister's hands slipped off the wood and he was gone, gone into the presence of Christ.

The man John spoke to survived, and some time later he stood in a pulpit and announced, "I am John Harper's last convert."

There is nothing more important than a personal relationship with Christ. We belong to God our Father. And when one of His children comes home, there is joy!

ENVY

Rebecca Manley Pippert,
writer

> " 'My son,' the father said, 'you are always with me,
> and everything I have is yours.
> But we had to celebrate and be glad,
> because this brother of yours was dead and is alive again;
> he was lost and is found.' "
>
> LUKE 15:31–32 NIV

The first stage of envy always begins with comparison. Indeed, it would be hard to imagine envy taking root on a planet with only one person. Envy takes two.

Because of envy, the elder brother in the story of the Prodigal Son couldn't celebrate his brother's miraculous return by coming to the welcome-home party. "You never gave a party like that for me!" Never mind that everything his father owned was already his. Envy was shouting, "No! I've been deprived. I got a raw deal, and I bitterly resent that my brother got preferential treatment."

The elder brother clearly illustrates how blind the envious are. They are blind to God's blessings in their lives, which makes them ungrateful, and they are blind to their own sin, which makes them self-righteous and proud. In the end, the cry and final logic of the envious is always, "I've been treated unjustly and somebody owes me!" It's a miserable way to live.

STICKS AND STONES

Jane Carr,
Christian education professor,
Biola University

Do not let any unwholesome talk come out of your mouths,
but only what is helpful for building others up according to
their needs, that it may benefit those who listen.

EPHESIANS 4:29 NIV

Sticks and stones may break my bones, but words will never hurt me." Yeah, right! It may sound like a great comeback, but in reality "words" have a way of cutting to the core. I was diagnosed with a condition called scoliosis, a curvature of the spine. As a result, I spent my first three years of high school in a full body brace that I had to wear twenty-three hours a day. The brace extended from my neck to my hips. Two steel rods ran on the backside and one on the front side, the three connecting with a steel-like collar that sat loosely around the neck.

Even though the brace was mostly covered by clothes, people couldn't help but notice it. In particular I remember leaving class one day and passing a guy in the hallway who commented, "Hey, Frankenstein, it's too early for Halloween." Ouch! A flippant remark, but deeply hurtful.

The words we say have the ability to tear down or build up. We tear down when we choose to have a critical spirit, use put-downs, or gossip. We build up when we choose to encourage, honor, and look for the best in others. The challenge is yours. . .watch your words!

BEING COURAGEOUS

Joy Mosbarger,
college professor

*"Be strong and courageous! Do not tremble or be dismayed,
for the LORD your God is with you wherever you go."*
JOSHUA 1:9 NASB

These are God's words to Joshua as he is about to embark on the task of taking possession of the land God had promised the Israelites. Although most of us will never have occasion to conquer a land as Joshua did, every day you face situations that require courage. What do you do if your biology teacher denies the possibility that God created the heavens and the earth? Or what do you do if everyone else at a party is drinking or taking drugs? In such cases, it can be difficult to say or do what is right. But courage does not necessarily mean you feel no twinges of fear about taking a stand. Rather it means that you take a stand in spite of that apprehension.

You can demonstrate courage and overcome fear because of the assurance that the Lord your God is with you wherever you go, whatever situation you face. When you're about to take a stand that you think will be unpopular, it helps to have a friend standing by your side. God will always be that friend, and His presence is an inexhaustible source of courage and strength.

LIVING SACRIFICES

Joni Eareckson Tada,
quadriplegic writer and speaker

*Therefore, I urge you, brothers, in view of God's mercy,
to offer your bodies as living sacrifices, holy and pleasing to God—
this is your spiritual act of worship.*

ROMANS 12:1 NIV

What immediately comes to mind when you hear the word "sacrifice"? Articles in *National Geographic* magazines about bloody offerings in Aztec temples? The streams running red with lamb's blood outside the temple of Jerusalem? Whatever comes to mind, it's probably not a pretty picture.

But sacrifice is what God asks of us. Living sacrifice. Now that tickles my imagination. I picture myself on an altar, and as soon as God strikes the match to light the flame of some fiery ordeal, I do what any living sacrifice would do. I crawl off the altar!

This is exactly the dilemma Christians face. First, we are to present our bodies, that is, give them in the Lord's service as a freewill offering. And because our sacrifice is a living one, it involves a choice. The gift of salvation does not require us to become a living sacrifice. . . . We are not forced onto the altar. . . . We are not coerced to stay on that altar. It is a choice we make out of love.

FOREVER FRIENDS

Deborah McIntire,
educator and writer

*"Do not merely look out for your own personal interests,
but also for the interests of others."*

PHILIPPIANS 2:4 NASB

Linda, Sheila, and I were inseparable through high school. Unfortunately, in our junior year, both Linda and Sheila had serious boyfriends and I did not. They began spending more and more time with their boyfriends, and I felt left out. I thought my friendship with them was no longer a priority to them.

Valentine's Day was approaching, and I was sad to even think of it. I knew they would both have special celebrations with their boyfriends, while I would be left at home alone. Much to my surprise, on Valentine's Day afternoon, both Linda and Sheila appeared at my door, ready to kidnap me for a fun afternoon of lunch and shopping. I couldn't believe it. I was touched by their thoughtfulness and kindness.

They told me, "We love you. You're important to us. And we are sorry that we have not spent as much time with you as we should have."

Throughout our high school years, we all had several boyfriends. However, we all learned that day the importance of spending time with each other. Though boyfriends came and went, we girlfriends remained close for years to come.

THE FIVE-FINGER DISCOUNT

Kristi Norton,
teacher

> *How blessed is the man who does not walk*
> *in the counsel of the wicked,*
> *Nor stand in the path of sinners.*
>
> PSALM 1:1 NASB

Even though there is no scriptural basis, I have always "ranked" sin. For instance, lying was not nearly as bad as stealing. However, how do you rank watching your friends steal and then not saying anything? That was the challenging place I found myself in during my freshman year. My non-Christian friends showed no remorse for taking whatever they wanted from the store—their "five-finger discount." Even though I was a Christian, I still found it difficult to stand up for what was right. After all, I didn't want to sound like a goody-goody. Unfortunately, the only solution I found helpful was to just walk away.

Recently, I found myself counseling a young girl who had gotten involved with drugs within her group of friends. She was afraid to stand up to the group for the same reason—not wanting to sound like a Christian snob. What I realize now is that you don't need to be ashamed of your Christianity and your desire to make good choices. Stealing, using drugs, and lying are all wrong. Thankfully, we have a God who loves us and wants to forgive us for all of our wrongdoing.

GOING IN CIRCLES

Beverly Plaugher,
writer

Let us also lay aside every encumbrance,
and the sin which so easily entangles us,
and let us run with endurance the race that is set before us,
fixing our eyes on Jesus, the author and perfecter of faith.

HEBREWS 12:1–2 NASB

Round and round, back and forth. . .in a circle again. We were trying to row away from the lakeshore so that we could meet two other campers in the next cove. However, we were going nowhere. Try as we may, we only rowed in awkward circles, never leaving the shore by more than fifteen feet. People along the shore began watching us and smiling. We changed positions in the rowboat, thinking that would help, but it didn't work. We continued rowing in the strange circular pattern in front of a gawking, growing crowd of amused onlookers. Finally, one little boy cried out, "If you take the rope off the rock, you'll go faster!" Ding! Ding! A flash of insight.

Red-faced and laughing hysterically, we finally managed to untie the boat from the rock and took off like Olympic rowers. We made it to the next cove just in time to meet the other campers.

Sometimes life is like rowing in circles instead of accomplishing our goals. You get nowhere until you let go of what is holding you back.

THANK YOU, LORD, FOR SEEING THE REAL ME

Anna Y. Wong,
early childhood director,
Sea Ridge Community Church

> "The LORD does not look at the things man looks at.
> Man looks at the outward appearance,
> but the LORD looks at the heart."
>
> 1 SAMUEL 16:7 NIV

Since first grade I was doomed to wearing glasses and living in a skinny body. My mother called me Four Eyes, and my sister called me Beanpole. My heavy Coke bottle glasses left an indentation on my nose and an impression on those around me.

At age seventeen, I purchased my first pair of contacts. Teachers and friends had to look twice before they recognized me. Even guys were interested in me now!

Now that I'm a little older, I've noticed almost everyone my age wears glasses and that glasses are in style. I'll sometimes wear my Coke bottles and am thankful my friends treat me the same. I've also become comfortable with my natural body weight.

It's comforting to know God sees our hearts. As time passes, the physical beauty may fade and wither, but the loveliness of one's heart for God will continue to shine through.

Thank You, Lord, for Your awesome love and for seeing the real me.

FINDING SIGNIFICANCE

Michelle L. Pecanic,
teacher

"The LORD your God is with you, he is mighty to save.
He will take great delight in you, he will quiet you with his love,
he will rejoice over you with singing."

ZEPHANIAH 3:17 NIV

There have been many times in my life when I have felt insignificant. From my limited human perspective, my friends and family had deserted me in these times, or at the very least, they had not lived up to my expectations, and I felt utterly alone.

But I have been reminded time and again that with God, we are never alone; we are not insignificant. God is with us, and He is mighty to save. . .from depression, despair, loneliness, and all the worries of this world, but most importantly from our sin that separates us from Him.

That is more than we deserve, but He doesn't stop there. Not only does He save us, but our mighty God delights in us and rejoices over us with singing despite our sins and failures of the past, present, and future. Stop and think about that. . .the God of the whole universe delights over us, His creation. We are not insignificant!

If you still doubt your significance, stop and silently listen for Him. . . . He promises to quiet you with His love. . . . Allow His peace and strength to wash over you. Praise Him for His loving care, and thank Him for making you a significant part of His plan.

GOD'S GLORY

Carrie Brown,
missionary to Southeast Asia

For with You is the fountain of life;
In Your light we see light.
PSALM 36:9 NASB

As I was driving, I turned a corner and was dazzled by the early morning sunrise. The sun's brightness shone directly into my eyes and everything else disappeared. As I drove on, I thought, *This must be something like being in the awesome glory of God's presence.*

Then, it was as if God spoke to me—this is what being in God's full presence will be like. We may not be able to see Him now, but when we see Him at last, all the troubles we thought were so big and important will fade away. We won't be able to see anything but God in His glory.

We may feel like God hides Himself from us at times, and the world may feel cold and dark—but when He reveals Himself to us, the memory of the night will fade away. We will be dazzled by His holiness and His glory. Our problems and cares will flee from our minds as we join together to worship the glorious One.

Come, Lord Jesus.

HOLES IN OUR HEARTS

Shelly Cunningham,
Christian education professor,
Biola University

Carry each other's burdens,
and in this way you will fulfill the law of Christ.

GALATIANS 6:2 NIV

I will be attending the funeral of a friend next week. Sitting up front will be her children—a high school girl, a junior high boy, and a third grader. I cry at the loss of my friend, but I cry more for her children, who now have a hole in their hearts.

When we lose someone in our life—through death, divorce, or a move, it often feels like we have a hole in our heart. Heart holes need friends who know the hole is there and who offer their hands to catch the tears that fall through it.

Galatians 6:2 tells us to carry each other's burdens. Do you have a hole in your heart? Do you know a friend who might have one? When we share a burden or carry a burden, we discover the hope of Christ right in the middle of the hole in the heart.

WATER BOTTLE WONDER

Sheila Walsh,
writer and recording artist

"Your Father knows what you need before you ask him."

MATTHEW 6:8 NIV

Helen Roseveare, [a] missionary doctor in Zaire, Africa, [has] told this amazing story:

"One night I had worked hard to help a mother in the labor ward; but in spite of all we could do, she died, leaving us with a tiny premature baby. We would have difficulty keeping the baby alive, as we had no incubator. A student midwife went to fill a hot-water bottle, [but while she was] filling the bottle, it burst. Rubber perishes easily in tropical climates. 'And this is our last hot-water bottle!' she lamented.

"The following noon I told [the orphanage children] about the baby. One ten-year-old girl, Ruth, prayed with her usual blunt conciseness. 'Please God,' she prayed, 'send us a water bottle. It'll be no good tomorrow, God, as the baby will be dead, so please send it this afternoon.'

"Halfway through the afternoon, I got a message that there was a car at my front door. By the time I had reached home, the car had gone, but there, on the veranda, was a parcel. Inside the package was a brand-new water bottle. That parcel had been on the way for five whole months."

WHO WANTS TO BE A GAZILLIONAIRE?

Martha Bolton,
writer

*Has not God chosen those who are poor in the eyes
of the world to be rich in faith and to inherit the kingdom
he promised those who love him?*

JAMES 2:5 NIV

Winning millions of dollars may sound nice on the surface, but having endless amounts of money comes at a price too. All of a sudden that person finds him- or herself with scores of friends. Often these are people who never gave that person the time of day before. All of a sudden, the millionaire is hearing from relatives he or she didn't even know existed. Money didn't solve this person's problems. It just created a whole new set of them.

Don't get me wrong. Money is nice. A full wallet is much more fun than one with only dust inside. Yet James warns us of the danger of putting riches before God. He reminds us that gold and silver (and savings accounts, new cars, CDs, and the latest fashions) are all temporary. They have absolutely no eternal value. They'll be like that cool new shirt we couldn't live without six years ago that we wouldn't be caught dead in today.

Money shouldn't determine our happiness. We need to be content, whether we have a lot or a little.

Money. It's going to be out of fashion in eternity.

PAIN

Carrie Purcell,
college student

My heart throbs, my strength fails me;
and the light of my eyes, even that has gone from me.
My loved ones and my friends stand aloof from my plague;
and my kinsmen stand afar off.
Those who seek my life lay snares for me;
and those who seek to injure me have threatened destruction,
and they devise treachery all day long.

PSALM 38:10–12 NASB

Pain is a part of the human life. It has many forms, and different people experience it differently. For some people, the presence of pain in the world is a significant problem for their faith. Pain's existence is not something God chooses to explain fully to us. However, how we should respond to it is made clear through the Scriptures.

First, we should be loving and compassionate toward other people who are in pain. No one's pain is irrelevant or unimportant. Judging the level of someone's suffering on a pain-o-meter and treating that person with that much compassion isn't right. Just because you think your day was worse than your sister's doesn't mean you shouldn't give her a chance to talk about her problems.

Second, one must have a proper attitude toward God. We have all asked God, "Why is this happening to me?" While anger with Him is natural at times, we must also remember that He is our loving Father, and there is a bigger reason for the pain that we are suffering.

JESUS, MY BEAUTY

Kathy Troccoli,
recording artist and writer

Those who look to him are radiant.

PSALM 34:5 NIV

Internal voices tell me I look horrible, fat, and un-attractive and that I always will. When I listen to these blows to my self-esteem, I let them crush my ability to see the truth of who God says I am, all He says I will become, all He desires for me, and all that He promised me. I am beautiful, lovely, and radiant only when I look to Him, only when I listen to His words and what He says about me. When, through obedience, I allow His character to become my charac-ter, He fills and covers all the holes of insecurity I've dug for myself.

Jesus is my beauty. He is my loveliness, my confi-dence. He is the charisma, the attractiveness that is right and true—that breeds life not death. That points to good and not evil. The perfume the world, our fam-ily, and our friends will take notice of. What is she wearing? Jesus. The answer must be Jesus.

INVITATIONS TO TEMPTATION?

Lorraine Peterson,
writer

Rather, clothe yourselves with the Lord Jesus Christ,
and do not think about how to gratify
the desires of the sinful nature.

ROMANS 13:14 NIV

A little boy who lived near a lake was instructed by his father never to go swimming without supervision. One day his father caught him swimming. Soon the innocent-sounding little guy was saying, "But, Daddy, I didn't mean to be swimming. It just happened."

"Then," replied his father, "why did you take your swimsuit with you when you came to play near the lake?"

The little boy answered, "I took it along just in case I got tempted."

Are you like that little boy? Do you devise plans that will make it harder for you to obey Jesus' commands, even though you say you love Him? Instead of providing yourself with the possibility for sinning, give yourself every opportunity to do right. If the little boy had left his swimsuit at home, the day would have ended differently.

Take Jesus with you through the day and think, "How would He plan for this situation?"

If you give yourself to Jesus, He'll show you how to organize your life so that obeying God's commandments will be easier.

UNFAILING THREADS

Gigi Graham Tchividjian,
writer and daughter of Billy Graham

For the word of God is living and active.
Sharper than any double-edged sword,
it penetrates even to dividing soul and spirit,
joints and marrow; it judges the thoughts
and attitudes of the heart.

HEBREWS 4:12 NIV

The Word of God is a living Word; it is the person of Jesus Christ, Himself, revealed to us. Psalm 119 says that the Word cleanses, strengthens, delights, teaches, saves, comforts, directs, and gives understanding. What a resource!

I am so grateful that I was taught early in my life to use this resource; to draw strength from it; to use it in seeking direction and guidance; to employ it in times of discouragement, disappointment, and loneliness.

There may come a day when we will no longer have the written Word of God. It is possible that it will have been taken away from us. But no one will ever be able to take away what we have hidden in our hearts and minds. Even if we do have our printed Bibles to refer to, reciting memorized Scripture is a simple way of abiding in God's Word all during the day.

Be sure to weave the unfailing threads of God's Word through the fabric of your heart and mind. It will hold strong, even if the rest of life unravels.

BEAUTY IS SOUL DEEP

99

HIDDEN PERSON OF THE HEART

Bonnie Saucy,
missionary in Kiev, Ukraine

Your adornment must not be merely external—braiding the hair,
and wearing gold jewelry, or putting on dresses;
but let it be the hidden person of the heart.

1 PETER 3:3–4 NASB

Before I got married, I made two decisions that I never regretted. They were: 1) I didn't need to marry a super good-looking guy, but I wanted to marry a guy who loved God and His Word. 2) I wanted to marry a guy that didn't just like my looks but, most of all, liked that I loved God and His Word. These two decisions have been the key ingredients in our marriage. I'll always remember the day when Mark, who is now my husband, told me that he was not only attracted to me, but most of all, he loved my heart for God. Whenever we have disagreements or difficulties, the problems have been solved because one or both of us have looked to God and His Word.

What kind of guy do you want to marry? Are you trying to attract him by just your outward appearance or also by a beautiful heart? Looks don't last, but the beautiful "hidden person of the heart" who loves God lasts forever.

You know what? God ended up giving me a very handsome husband. And he grows more and more handsome to me because of his love for God. And as my heart becomes more beautiful as I love God more, it shows on the outside as well.

FORGIVENESS

Dr. Kathryn Thompson Presley,
writer and retired teacher

*When my father and my mother forsake me,
then the LORD will take me up.*

PSALM 27:10 KJV

My mother's face contorted with rage. "You're no good! You'll never amount to anything!"

At sixteen, I'd learned to expect her tirades, for she was often depressed. She didn't mean everything she said. Still, her angry words wounded deeply.

Later that night, I lay very still and wished for death. Who would miss me? My little sister was too young. My father was too busy trying to support us.

Picking up the Bible my grandparents had given me, I noticed verses they had highlighted. There were verses in Proverbs 3 (NIV) that began: "Trust in the LORD with all your heart." With nothing much to lose, I whispered, "I *will* trust You."

Waves of liquid love swept through my spirit. Nothing much changed in outward circumstances, but I now had the "peace that passes all understanding." It carried me through my high school years, through college, through the demanding years of marriage, children, and establishing a career.

My mother and I were never close, but I had compassion for her—and forgave her before she died. Now, I look back to those early years and realize, "There hath not failed one word of His good promises."

THE MOST BEAUTIFUL PERSON

Heather Whitestone McCallum,
former Miss America,
with Angela Hunt

Charm is deceptive, and beauty is fleeting;
but a woman who fears the LORD is to be praised.

PROVERBS 31:30 NIV

About personal beauty—people often tell me that I am more beautiful in person than in my photographs or on television. I am flattered by the compliment, but I know they are saying that because when people see my face and figure in a picture, they are only seeing the outer shell. When they meet me, I think they catch a glimpse of Jesus inside me, and He is the most beautiful person in all the universe. If I am beautiful in person, it's because Jesus lights my eyes and sparks my smile. He is the gracefulness of my hands, the spring in my step, the lightness of my legs. The Bible says:

How beautiful on the mountains
are the feet of those who bring good news,
who proclaim peace,
who bring good tidings,
who proclaim salvation,
who say to Zion,
"Your God reigns!" (Isaiah 52:7 NIV)

I love that verse—even my battered ballet feet are beautiful when I'm dancing for God's glory!

GOD IS FAITHFUL. . .FOREVER

Jennifer Knapp,
recording artist

*No temptation has seized you except what is common
to man. And God is faithful; he will not let you
be tempted beyond what you can bear.
But when you are tempted, he will also provide
a way out so that you can stand up under it.*

1 CORINTHIANS 10:13 NIV

Have you ever found it hard to believe that Jesus did what He did on the cross? I have. I don't think God really expects us to fully comprehend it—just to believe it and accept the freedom Jesus' death and resurrection provides.

Life is full of many opportunities to live outside of God's desires for us—to sin, to disobey, to give in to temptation. What we do with those opportunities is what makes the difference between having a life full of joy or a life of frustration. God, in His infinite wisdom, knows that we face trials and temptations.

And God, in that infinite wisdom, gives us the ability to stand up under those trials and temptations.

In my own life, I have noticed that when I am walking closely with God and listening to Him, He gives me the words to say, the moves to make, and the wisdom to act in a way that is beyond my experience. I love it when that happens! Even though I am a sinful person, God is always faithful to help me rise above and beyond the pressures of the world in which I live.

BETTER THAN I THOUGHT

Gigi Graham Tchividjian,
writer and daughter of Billy Graham

> *To him who is able to keep you from falling*
> *and to present you before his glorious presence*
> *without fault and with great joy.*
>
> JUDE 24 NIV

The story is told of a certain Italian painter who lost some of his artistic skill as he grew older. One evening he sat discouraged before a canvas he had just completed. He was painfully aware that it didn't burst with life as had his former paintings. As he climbed the stairs to bed, his son heard him mumbling to himself, "I have failed. I have failed."

Later that evening the son, also an artist, went into the studio. He set to work, adding a touch of color here, a shadow there, a few highlights, greater depth. He continued far into the night, until at last the canvas fulfilled the old master's vision.

When morning came, the aging artist entered the studio to examine the work once again. He stood amazed before the perfected canvas and exclaimed in utter delight, "Ah, I have wrought better than I thought!"

The day will come when we will look upon the canvas of our lives, and through the transforming power of Christ, we will be amazed to discover that we too fulfill our heavenly Father's original vision.

Take heart! Remember. . .it is not about us, but about His glory.

SURRENDER

Elisabeth Elliot,
writer and missionary

*Then he said to them all: "If anyone would come
after me, he must deny himself and take up
his cross daily and follow me."*

LUKE 9:23 NIV

C an we give up all for the love of God? When the surrender of ourselves seems too much to ask, it is first of all because our thoughts about God Himself are paltry. We have not really seen Him; we have hardly tested Him at all and learned how good He is. In our blindness we approach Him with suspicious reserve. We ask how much of our fun He intends to spoil, how much He will demand from us, how high is the price we must pay before He is placated.

If we had the least notion of His loving-kindness and tender mercy, His fatherly care for His poor children, His generosity, His beautiful plans for us, if we knew how patiently He waits for our turning to Him, how gently He means to lead us to green pastures and still waters, how carefully He is preparing a place for us, how ceaselessly He is ordering and ordaining and engineering His Master Plan for our good—if we had any inkling of all this, could we be reluctant to let go of our smashed dandelions or whatever we clutch so fiercely in our sweaty little hands?

SEEING BOTH SIDES

Dianne E. Butts,
writer

But everyone must be quick to hear,
slow to speak and slow to anger.

JAMES 1:19 NASB

As Mom and I drove through South Dakota on vacation, we visited a wildlife area. A man at the top of a hill squatted, steadying a camera. Nearby him stood a sign, its skinny edge toward me. I walked up the hill and around to one side to read the sign. ENTIRE AREA GROUNDHOG COLONY, it read.

"They're kind of cute, aren't they?" I asked. The man gave me a puzzled look.

"They're dangerous," he said. "If they stomp their feet, it's a warning they're about to charge."

"Charge?" I thought. "A groundhog?"

Just then. . .*thum, thum.* A deep sound—that kind you feel more than you hear—thumped behind me.

Thum, thum. I felt the ground pulse beneath my feet. The man slowly rose and moved behind the sign. Ever so slowly, I peeked over my shoulder. Only a few yards behind me stood one huge buffalo.

Very slowly, I moved around behind the sign too. That's when I saw the other side of the sign, which held information and warnings about the buffalo in the area!

When I have found myself miscommunicating with a friend, I have learned to stop and find out what the other side says.

DID I SAY THAT?

La Verne Tolbert, Ph.D.,
psychologist and writer

Out of the same mouth proceed blessing and cursing.
My brethren, these things ought not to be so.
JAMES 3:10 NKJV

Lorraine ran upstairs to her room and slammed her bedroom door. The crash was so hard that it shook the entire house. Throwing herself onto her bed, she beat the pillows, screaming over and over, "I hate her!"

Hours later, her dad knocked on her bedroom door. "May I come in?"

Lorraine turned away from his gaze.

"You said very ugly words to your mother, and that's unacceptable."

Lorraine was embarrassed and almost asked herself out loud, "Did I say that?"

Christian young women have the same challenges with their mothers that other girls face, but there should be a difference in how a believer responds when angry. It's never the right decision to hurt someone else by lashing out at them with our words. The biblical writer, James, asks us an important question. "Does a spring send forth fresh water and bitter from the same opening?" What we say when we're angry (or when we stub a toe. . .or miss the last bus) tells what's really deep inside of us. It takes prayer for wisdom to stop and think before we speak. And it takes practice to learn to respond correctly.

BEAUTY IS SOUL DEEP

POWER DRAIN

Carla Perez,
pastor's wife, chauffeur to four sons

*Let us also lay aside every encumbrance and the sin which so easily
entangles us, and let us run with endurance the race
that is set before us, fixing our eyes on Jesus.*

HEBREWS 12:1–2 NASB

One cold, rainy afternoon, shortly after I had gotten my license, I was out driving in a storm. Traffic slowed to a crawl through large pools of water. In one section, several cars stalled in knee-deep water. I cautiously entered the area, prayerfully inched forward, and successfully emerged on the other side.

Then came the hill. My car slowed and almost stopped. I gave it more gas. No change. I turned off the radio to better hear the engine—it revved a little. I was curious. I turned off the heater. More power. I turned off the defroster. Even more power. By the time I had turned off the wipers, the car easily moved up the hill. I had to stop everything that drained energy from my car battery and refocus the power on the car's primary purpose.

I think about the rainy day my car almost stalled when I get too busy and start feeling swamped. Maybe I'm doing too many things. Maybe I'm draining my car battery. When I refocus on Christ's power and drop unnecessary activities, I reenergize and life moves forward more smoothly.

Lord, fill me with Your energy and help me accomplish Your purposes.

MY IDENTITY

Tina C. Elacqua, Ph.D.,
assistant professor,
Crichton College

*So God created humankind in his image, in the image of God
he created them; male and female he created them.*

GENESIS 1:27 NRSV

Have you ever felt like you just didn't fit in with the popular crowd at school or perhaps even in your own family? I didn't grow up in a Christian home. I had three older siblings who continually told me lies about who I was. My siblings were insistent that I wasn't Mom and Pop's daughter. They taunted me because of my blond hair and blue eyes, which was not the norm for our Italian family. At times, I felt like a stranger—an alien in my own home.

My siblings were right—I didn't fit in, not because I looked different, but because I had the Spirit of God living inside me. If you have accepted Jesus Christ as your Lord and Savior, then you too have the Spirit of God living in you (1 Corinthians 2:12; 2 Corinthians 1:22; Ephesians 1:13). You have the mind of Christ (1 Corinthians 2:16), and your body is a temple of the Holy Spirit (1 Corinthians 6:19). You no longer need to feel like a stranger and alien because you are God's daughter. What better place to fit in than as a member in the family of God (Ephesians 2:19)?

A Lesson in Humility

Diane Guido,
associate dean,
Azusa Pacific University

> *"Whoever exalts himself shall be humbled; and*
> *whoever humbles himself shall be exalted."*
>
> MATTHEW 23:12 NASB

Being a cheerleader had been a dream for me. As a high school sophomore, I was shy and inexperienced in cheer—an unlikely candidate for the squad. But I tried out anyway.

For the first round of competition, I smiled nervously for the judges, yelling for the Knights as I performed the required routines. When the results were posted, I inched my way up to the front of the line of girls, straining to read the small print. Just as I got close enough to recognize my name, I heard someone say with a tone of disgust, "Diane. . .who is that?" My heart sank. I clearly was not popular. That did not bode well for the final round of the competition, the popular vote.

For days, I pondered that question: "Who is that?" I wondered who I really was and whether popularity was what I was seeking. My soul-searching led me to realize that popularity is not important in God's plan. What a lesson in humility for me! And in a surprise twist, I did become a cheerleader that year—a grateful and certainly a more humble cheerleader.

THE HIGHEST CALLING

Twila Paris,
recording artist

Your attitude should be the same as that of Christ Jesus:
Who, being in very nature God, did not consider equality with God
something to be grasped, but made himself nothing,
taking the very nature of a servant, being made in human likeness.
And being found in appearance as a man, he humbled himself
and became obedient to death—even death on a cross!

PHILIPPIANS 2:5–8 NIV

At Youth with a Mission [YWAM] in Arkansas, we have a ministry-wide picnic every September—usually at one of the nearby lakes. Everyone spends the day swimming, boating, hiking, and taking part in all sorts of organized games and activities, including eating! Everyone, that is, except the ministry leaders. They spend the day grilling hamburgers and hot dogs for almost three hundred people, cleaning up after them, and doing all the other necessary tasks. They spend the day literally serving those they lead, an attitude of the heart that is evident in their lives year-round.

So often we tend to look down on positions of service—setting our sights, instead, on higher positions that appear to bring with them privilege, authority, and respect. What we forget is that Jesus Himself chose to be a servant, and the greatest privilege we can have is following His example. To lay down our rights, our ambitions, and our lives in obedience to the Father is actually the highest calling in the Kingdom of God.

TRUTH OR DARE?

Cherie Fresonke,
missionary and writer in Bulgaria

The one who sows to please his sinful nature,
from that nature will reap destruction;
the one who sows to please the Spirit,
from the Spirit will reap eternal life.

GALATIANS 6:8 NIV

Have you ever played the game "Truth or Dare"? As a Christian teenager, I had no idea that I was playing that game. Unfortunately, I had not taken the time to get to know my Savior as a personal friend nor did I read His Word. Because of this, I was focused on my sinful nature and the things of the world—playing a game without realizing it.

At sixteen I discovered I was pregnant. I chose once again to live a dare when I decided to have an abortion. Soon my life was out of control. No one told me when I began to play this game that it would lead to depression and anxiety, drugs and alcohol, or thoughts of suicide.

But we have a wonderful God who is rich in mercy. The moment I returned to Him to live by the truth, He forgave me and washed my sin away. In fact, He took my guilt and shame and now uses it for His glory. I work in both America and eastern Europe, teaching the truth of His love to teenagers like you. So, which will it be—truth or dare?

SPIRITUAL WHITE-OUT

Barbara Johnson,
Women of Faith speaker and writer

"Though your sins are as scarlet, they will be as white as snow."
ISAIAH 1:18 NASB

Many years ago I had a job scheduling doctor's appointments. When someone would cancel or reschedule, the marks would make the book look messy. That bothered me. . . . Then one day I discovered that White-Out was the miracle I'd been looking for to keep the doctor's books orderly and professional looking. I'd paint a nice clean space where the client's name had been. At the end of the day, every page was neat and clean. Instead of messy columns, there'd be straight and easy-to-read names for the receptionist in the office.

I used to call White-Out my 1 John 1:9* stuff because it would blot out the mess and leave a clean place—just like God does with our sins. We all need that spiritual White-Out to make us white as snow. It reminds us we can all have a clean fresh start every day. Every dawn is a new beginning. . . . No, we can't go back and change the past, but God can make each space in our lives new. One thing God cannot see is our sin because it is covered by His special White-Out: the blood of Jesus.

* "If we confess our sins, He is faithful and righteous to forgive us our sins, and to cleanse us from all unrighteousness" (1 John 1:9 NASB).

Being Friendly

La Verne Tolbert, Ph.D.,
psychologist and writer

A man who has friends must himself be friendly.
PROVERBS 18:24 NKJV

Tamika *thinks she's so cool,* Sarah thought as she watched Tamika arrive to the youth group. It seemed that everyone wanted to be Tamika's friend. *It's only because she knows the latest dance steps and dresses great,* thought Sarah disdainfully.

"Okay, let's get started," announced Pastor Bob. "Tonight's lesson is from Proverbs. 'A man who has friends must himself be friendly.' I watched you arrive tonight to see how friendly you were to one another. Some went out of their way to talk, while others stood in the shadows. We assume that people don't want to be our friends, but we never stop to ask, 'Why?' If a person doesn't even know you, then how can they dislike you?"

Sarah was nearly in tears. She wanted friends. Out of nowhere, Tamika appeared.

"Hey, Sarah. We're starting a new group and we're one person short. Can you help us out?"

"I thought you didn't like me, but you're asking me to be a part of your group?"

"Well, I thought you didn't like me either," replied Tamika. "But I decided to do what Pastor Bob suggested and 'show myself friendly.' " After a long pause, they both started laughing.

RESOURCEFULNESS

Diane Guido,
associate dean,
Azusa Pacific University

The plans of the diligent lead surely to advantage.

PROVERBS 21:5 NASB

Choosing a college can be fraught with many challenges. I struggled with that decision, unsure of my major, whether to go far from home, what environment would be best, and how to pay for it.

As one of four children of hardworking parents with limited resources, the financial question loomed largest. Despite my father's cautions to be realistic about my college choice, I determined not to allow financial concerns to become the overriding factor in where I would attend.

With the help and support of counselors and librarians, I applied for many scholarships and grants—no award was too small; no application was too daunting. And as I received the results of those applications, I was pleased to see that the hard work had paid off: I had at least two workable college choices!

Perhaps I was not blessed with a lot of money as a teenager. But I believe God blessed me with resourcefulness. In some ways, it was using that resourcefulness in the "small things"—focusing on the many details in the financial aid applications—that resulted in the "many things"—increased opportunities later on. Hard work and faithfulness to one's gifts can indeed pay off.

Beauty and the Feast Beast

Nancy C. Anderson,
writer, speaker, and former teenager

> *Your body is a temple of the Holy Spirit....*
> *Glorify God in your body.*
>
> 1 Corinthians 6:19–20 nasb

I asked the girl sitting next to me at our senior banquet, "How can you eat so much and still stay so skinny? You have been back to the buffet table at least four times!" She replied, "If you'll wait until I'm finished eating these desserts, and you promise to keep my secret, I'll show you."

I watched her gobble down a piece of apple pie, two doughnuts, and a cookie. Then she said, "Follow me." We walked into the rest room, and she went into the stall. She said, "Watch this." I started to watch, but then I looked away. She was throwing up!

I had always admired Sheri. She was a blond cheerleader with waist-long hair and a yearlong tan. She was beautiful. But my opinion of her changed that day. She wasn't beautiful when she came out of that bathroom stall. Her desire to be "perfect" had driven her to abuse her body and risk her health, and I felt sorry for her.

TRUTH OR CONSEQUENCE?

June Hetzel,
education professor,
Biola University

And he who tells lies will not escape.

PROVERBS 19:5 NASB

I really wanted to go to Mary Jo's house for lunch, but my mother said, "No." So, Mary Jo and I hatched a lamebrain plan to sneak over to her house and enjoy a lunch together anyway.

Mary Jo's mom prepared a delicious meal for us—sandwiches, chips, and our favorite drink. When her mother asked if I had permission to be there, I happily cooed, "Oh, yes!"

We munched on yummy sandwiches, laughed, and told jokes, until about twenty minutes into the fun, the phone rang. My heart sank.

"Oh, really?" Mary Jo's mother said in a low tone. It took a split second for me to assess the situation, slither from my lunch seat, and bolt out the door. I ran down the street and into my own house. There was my mother, still on the phone. She had the same "killer" look in her eyes as Mary Jo's mom. I learned right then and there that "[s]he who tells lies will not escape."

WHAT WAS GOD THINKING?

La Verne Tolbert, Ph.D.,
psychologist and writer

I will give thanks to You, for I am fearfully and wonderfully made;
wonderful are Your works, and my soul knows it very well.

PSALM 139:14 NASB

During her first week at a new foster home, Annette woke up with a breakout. "Great. I'm out of medicine and, look, another pimple! What on earth was God thinking when He made me?"

Edith, her foster mother, immediately understood. "You're under a lot of stress. Hormones are jumping around. We'll find the right medication after school."

A new prescription and encouraging words from the doctor helped Annette feel a little better. Still, she felt God was picking on her.

"When I was your age, I had the same problem," Edith confessed. Annette could hardly believe her ears. She was looking into a face with beautiful, smooth skin. "As our bodies develop, hormones seem to go haywire, but soon they settle down." She handed Annette an index card. "I wrote this verse for you to put on your bathroom mirror. Read it aloud. Who you are inside is not dependent upon how you look outside. God loves you, Annette."

"I am fearfully and wonderfully made." Annette realized that God did care about her after all. Of all the homes in which she could have been placed, her foster mother, Edith, had understood her. This in itself was a small miracle.

FACING RESPONSIBILITY

Paula Miller,
English professor,
Biola University

The naïve inherit foolishness,
But the sensible are crowned with knowledge.

PROVERBS 14:18 NASB

When I was sixteen, my mother went to the hospital to give birth to my youngest brother. Although our grandmother offered to supervise our household in my mother's absence, I convinced my parents that I, as the capable, oldest daughter, could handle three days of preparing meals and supervising my siblings after school. Really, how hard could it be?

Everything went fine until the second day, when I discovered a mouse trapped in a tall trashcan stored in a dark cubbyhole beneath the kitchen stairs. The furry creature was trying to jump out of the container and was within inches of succeeding.

I detested mice, and the realization that the rodent might escape made me want to run, but I could not. I had responsibilities. I consulted my ten-year-old brother, who advised putting a cat into the trashcan, so it could get the mouse. His plan proved disastrous. The cat became frightened, overturned the container, and both creatures escaped.

The humorous incident taught me that childish advice yields childish consequences. A mature individual cannot expect others to solve her problems for her. Rather than relying on God to help me face my irrational fear, I had surrendered my responsibility to a ten year old.

IMMEASURABLY MORE

Debrah Jay Smith,
Young Life area director,
Huntington Beach, California

Now to him who is able to do immeasurably
more than all we ask or imagine,
according to his power that is at work within us,
to him be glory in the church
and in Christ Jesus throughout all generations, for ever and ever!

EPHESIANS 3:20–21 NIV

While growing up, my favorite board game was the game of "Life." It's a great game—lots of fun! For instance, you take a chance at the wheel, and you soon win a million dollars, receive a spouse, twins, and a new car. You retire in some cottage and live happily ever after.

As a young girl, I thought that was exactly how my own life was going to go. Until, that is, my sister died of cancer when I was seventeen.

If it weren't for my relationship with God, I would not have made it through, and I certainly would not have been able to recognize God in the midst of a very chaotic and painful time. For the first time ever, it became clear to me that when God is the one spinning the wheel of our lives, His plan for our future and our lives far exceeds that of any board game. We may experience great loss and pain, but we have a hope and a confidence in God. He dreams for each of our lives in ways we could never even imagine for ourselves—and with that confidence we are sure to win!

BRINGING FRAGRANCE INTO THE WORLD

Sheila Walsh,
writer and recording artist

*But thanks be to God, who always leads us in triumphal procession
in Christ and through us spreads everywhere
the fragrance of the knowledge of him.*

2 CORINTHIANS 2:14 NIV

September 11 has become a day that will forever stand alone in our calendar. For many it was a wakeup call to the reality that evil exists in our world. For those of us who love and trust God, it was a reminder that our enemy is not simply in human form, but he is a constant spiritual reality, one who roams around seeking whom he may destroy.

For too long in our nation, the Church has been defined by what we stand against. It is time to show in whose lovely name we come with arms stretched out to love. As we will never forget this day, let us never forget that other day of utter barbarism when the Lamb of God took on Himself the worst that hell had to throw at Him. He did it for you and for me. He did it so that we could be free. There will be a day when every knee will bow and every tongue confess that Jesus Christ is Lord. Until that day, we bring His fragrance to a world that has lost hope, that has lost heart. In His name we come.

THE BEAUTY OF FORGIVENESS

Heather Whitestone McCallum,
former Miss America,
with Angela Hunt

Be kind and compassionate to one another, forgiving each other,
just as in Christ God forgave you.

EPHESIANS 4:32 NIV

There are times when the Spirit of God pricks my conscience, and I am horrified by the selfishness in my own life. Yet my sin is the basis of my love for God. How could I not love the one who forgave so much?

When I look at those who hurt me, I cannot help but think of how richly my life has been saturated with forgiveness. And when I extend my hand in mercy, the sweet aroma of God's grace wafts over those around me, and they are blessed too.

If a secret sin haunts your life, confess it today— and be surprised by the incredible wealth of God's forgiveness.

If you have withheld forgiveness in order to nurse an old wound, know that you can find healing and release in that same wealth.

Finally, if there is some sin you cannot forgive yourself, remember that if God can forgive, so can you.

Forgive—and let God surprise you with His amazing love!

TRUSTING IN A
STRESS-FREE GOD

Brittany Waggoner,
college student and writer

Cast all your anxiety on him because he cares for you.
1 PETER 5:7 NIV

Worry does tear us apart. When my mother doesn't have something to worry about, she will worry that she is missing something and worry anyway! Piling up more and more worries about things that could happen is like loading up a van that doesn't have tires. The worries aren't going anywhere; they are just sitting there.

When we do lay our problems at God's feet, we can finally sit back and relax. Unfortunately, we often have the wrong perspective. We think that at the end of the day, when we tell God all our problems, we can climb into a comfy chair and relax. I think "casting our cares" should be more like a comfortable coat that we wear everywhere we go. Relaxing into God's loving care can be something we do all day long.

Stress is a part of life. There will be times of little stress and times when you have nothing but stress! However, no matter how much stress you have, God remains the same. He is consistently bigger than any of your problems or worries. Unlike you and me, He is thoroughly stress-free and waiting to give us peace in the midst of our chaos.

WHEN YOU KNOW YOU ARE RIGHT

Kathy McReynolds,
college professor

*The very fact that you have lawsuits among you means you have
been completely defeated already. Why not rather be wronged?*

1 CORINTHIANS 6:7 NIV

Not too long ago, a friend and I were working out together at the gym. We were having a very interesting conversation when all of a sudden the discussion became awkward and heated. Before I knew it, she was running out of the gym crying. How could this happen? To tell the truth, I'm not really sure what happened in those few moments when words were flying between us. But I knew one thing for sure: I was right! And that was all that was important. . .to me.

Well, the apostle Paul sees things a little differently. He asks, "Why not rather be wronged?" "Why not rather be cheated?" The point Paul seems to be making in this passage is that when you have a dispute with your brother or sister, what is important is not that you know you are right, but that you are right with who you know. We who are disciples of Christ must be in right relationship with each other. This is what is important. The world watches to see how we treat each other. So we must beware. Being "right" is not what matters most. In God's Kingdom "rightness" is not measured by the strength of an argument, but by the quality of our relationships. I quickly apologized to my friend, and thankfully she forgave me.

KNITTING TOGETHER FRIENDSHIPS

Anne and Ray Ortlund,
speakers and writers

*The soul of Jonathan was knit with the soul of David,
and Jonathan loved him as his own soul.*

1 SAMUEL 18:1 KJV

Aren't there people you'd like to have your heart knit to? You think of those with whom you'd be thrilled to have a David-Jonathan friendship.

But knitting takes time. It takes time for a bone to knit. It takes time for a sweater to be knit. It takes time for a friendship to be knit.

May this fact give you pause, but not stop you. It probably means you can't have dozens of good friends, but give enough time in your life for at least two or three.

Everyone needs really close friends. God made you for that. Paul prayed that believers might be "comforted, being knit together in love" (Colossians 2:2 KJV).

Investing enough time for lives to knit together means developing patience. In the Scriptures, "patience" is often translated "longsuffering," which gives you a better idea. To become a good friend means to learn to put up with a lot—cheerfully, because it's worth it.

To have a deep, rich friendship takes patience. We all need to take the time to hear each other out, to consider each other's viewpoints, to pray, to wait, to soften.

Feeling Like a Nobody in a Somebody World

Debbie Graham,
writer

But by the grace of God I am what I am.
1 Corinthians 15:10 NIV

Every day many voices try to shape your identity. The world has its voices, and God has His own. What voices are shaping you? Do you ever feel that you fall short in your own eyes or don't measure up to others' expectations? (If only I had a better personality, a better body, were more talented, etc.) Do you feel that you don't fit in? (If only I had more friends, a boyfriend, a car, great clothes, more freedom, etc.) Are you tempted to give up on you?

God wants you to tune out the chattering voices of the world and move forward with His voice right into the panoramic view of how He sees you.

God says, when he looks at you, he sees *somebody* holy, *somebody* chosen, and *somebody* dearly loved. he sees *somebody* who has not only been made right with him but who has been made *perfect* (can you believe it?) through the blood of jesus. he says you're *somebody* who shares a heavenly calling with him. he says you're *somebody* who can come boldly to Him when you're in need.

If the creator and ruler of the universe views you as all that, who are you to argue?

FORGIVING OTHERS

Quin Sherrer and Ruthanne Garlock,
writers

*"In your anger do not sin": Do not let the sun go down while you
are still angry, and do not give the devil a foothold. Get rid of
all bitterness, rage and anger, brawling and slander, along with
every form of malice. Be kind and compassionate to one another,
forgiving each other, just as in Christ God forgave you.*

EPHESIANS 4:26–27, 31–32 NIV

Satan attacks our capacity to give and receive forgiveness. He provokes us to indulge our grievances
and hold on to our bitterness by telling us over and
over, "The person who did this to you doesn't deserve
to be forgiven!"

What fruit does unforgiveness bear? It keeps us in
bondage to hurts and memories of the past. It stifles
joy and poisons relationships. It even makes us suscep-
tible to physical illnesses.

In Paul's letters, he cautioned believers against
harboring unforgiveness toward others, because it
opens a door to the enemy.

The negative behavior and attitudes mentioned all
have to do with human relationships. Paul was writing
to Christians here, but it is clear by his language that
they needed to deal with the grievances and hard feelings they had toward one another. He reminds them
that forgiving each other, following Christ's example, is
the solution to their conflicts as well as their protection
against the devil's strategy. And it's our protection too.

UNFADING BEAUTY

Darlene Peterson,
writer

You should be known for the beauty that comes from within,
the unfading beauty of a gentle and quiet spirit,
which is so precious to God.

1 PETER 3:4 NLT

Chung Himple, Mrs. Washington America, learned the secret of unfading beauty while growing up.

Chung was born to an American father and a Korean mother who met during the Korean War. While she enjoyed being a part of two cultures, when an American school bully taunted her, Chung's spirit was crushed by feelings of inferiority.

Later, when Chung made the all-important decision to accept Jesus' loving sacrifice on the cross for her sins, God's love lessened Chung's inferior feelings.

But as a teen, a skin irritation on her arms and legs subjected her again to ridicule. Fragile feelings gave way to faith when Chung realized God accepted her unconditionally, even with these skin irritations.

Now Chung wanted to "be what God made her, inside and out." Her interest grew to serving others, and it was her desire to be a "wish-grantor" for sick children that led to her interest in beauty pageants.

Chung's inner beauty continues to touch the world with God's love. In this day of hype about outward appearance, it is refreshing to know a woman whose beauty is more than "skin-deep."

GRACE GIVERS

Thelma Wells,
speaker and writer

*From the fullness of his grace we have all received
one blessing after another.*
JOHN 1:16 NIV

I really believe that the way people treat us is usually a direct result of how we treat them. I've watched it. When I go into a store looking preoccupied and unfriendly, I get that same treatment from the workers. If I smile, speak to them, and treat them with respect, I usually get the same treatment. It's called reciprocal response.

How do people treat you when you are shopping or needing service? If you are getting poor service, maybe you are bringing with you an appearance or action that causes others to back off from you or to treat you with a long-handled spoon.

A good attitude and a warm smile, a friendly hand-shake, or a sincere compliment wins half the battle in all our relationships. When service is shoddy, you can change the atmosphere with kindness. Do not recipro-cate negatively! Grace is what God gives us when our attitudes are bad. And grace we should freely give.

FREE MEANS FREE

Martha Bolton,
writer

> *Humbly accept the word planted in you,*
> *which can save you.*
> JAMES 1:21 NIV

Do you find yourself going in dozens of different circles just trying to get everything done that you need to get done "for the Lord"? If you're keeping this kind of schedule in order to earn God's love, then you're trying to do the impossible and the unnecessary. None of us has to earn God's love. We can't go to enough church services, help out with enough youth meetings, sell enough candy bars, or rock enough babies in the church nursery to earn what God has already given to us.

If we're so busy doing "God's business" that we're bitter and miserable, complaining every chance we get about all the things we have "to do for the Lord," then we're working for the wrong reasons. Again, James is asking us to check our motives. God wants our service to be true service, not drudgery. He wants our faithfulness to be true faithfulness, not a feeling of being trapped in an obligation. He wants our works to come naturally, out of a love for Him.

The Abundant Life

Kathy Troccoli,
recording artist and writer

Love must be sincere.

ROMANS 12:9 NIV

I am humbled when I read how God wants me to treat others, and I know I need to grow in my heart's capacity to love in a way that puts others above myself. What if you and I were videotaped for at least a week—every day, all day—at home, at work, at play—and then the video played back for our church, family, friends, anyone who looks up to us? Would we talk and act differently? Would we live differently? Does the very thought of a daily videotape send shivers up your spine? It would show so much about how we live and who we are living for.

The truth is that God is watching. He is aware. Not with a gigantic teaching stick in one hand and a check-off list in the other, but with eyes that see to our very core—eyes desiring that we live in the riches of His grace so that we may be able to eat of the good fruit that comes from a life rooted in love. Now that is the abundant life.

SEEKING WISE COUNSELORS

Brittany Waggoner,
college student and writer

For waging war you need guidance,
and for victory many advisers.

PROVERBS 24:6 NIV

You and I might not be going off to battle in a true military sense. Yet the struggles of life often feel like a type of war, and we can benefit a lot from the wisdom of the people we love and trust.

Think of all the people around you at school, at church, in your neighborhood, and in your family. All have had unique experiences that have taught them a great deal. If your loved ones are given an opportunity to share the wisdom they have gained through hard times, then in a very real way, their pain was worth it. You can enrich the lives of those people, young or old, by giving them an opportunity to share the lessons God has taught them. You can also benefit from their wisdom.

Whether friends or family, leaders or mentors, the advice of God's people will give you the guidance you want and need to make your tough decisions.

WHAT DO YOU THINK?

Carol Baker,
secretary to the dean,
Talbot School of Theology

*Finally, brethren, whatever is true, whatever is honorable,
whatever is right, whatever is pure, whatever is lovely,
whatever is of good repute, if there is any excellence and
if anything worthy of praise, dwell on these things.*

PHILIPPIANS 4:8 NASB

You've heard it said that feelings are neither right nor wrong, they just are; but is that really true? Could it be that your feelings are actually a result or outpouring of what you're thinking? How do you feel? Are you happy or sad? Are you worried or anxious? Are you angry or resentful?

Take a few minutes from time to time to examine yourself to see what has influenced you lately. What have you been reading? What have you seen at the movies or watched on TV? How is your relationship with your parents and your friends? What do you talk about? Everything in your life influences your thoughts; and your thoughts influence how you feel, how you act, and what you say. Examine yourself to see how much of your time is spent reading, studying, and meditating on God's Word. Are you allowing enough time for God to influence you through His Word? What do you think?

SINKING SAND

Sherrie Murphree,
teacher

> "Therefore everyone who hears these words of Mine
> and acts on them, may be compared to a wise man
> who built his house on the rock."
>
> MATTHEW 7:24 NASB

My family of four visited the sand dunes at the state park right outside of Monahans, Texas. Not until that time did the "sinking sand" phrase from the old hymn, "The Solid Rock," have so much significance.

The vastness of sand in all directions was awesome. It excited a spirit of freedom in me. Barefoot, walking—trudging rather, up and down the dunes, I felt like a little girl whose dream of her own giant sandbox had come true.

A worshipful quiet cloaked the dunes, and the sun baked the grains. My toes squeezed deeper into the sand, reaching for some cool relief. We caravanned across the top of the dunes. I stopped and looked back to see the blizzardlike wind erasing all traces of human footprints.

God reminded me that all of life's pursuits without Christ as the foundation are sinking sand, just like my footprints that disappeared in the blizzardlike wind. However, when I build my life upon the solid Rock, the heaviest, most torrential winds can never shake my firm foundation in Christ.

GOD HAS A PLAN FOR ME

Misty Bernall,
mother of teen martyr Cassie Bernall

" 'For I know the plans that I have for you,'
declares the LORD, 'plans for welfare and not
for calamity to give you a future and a hope.' "

JEREMIAH 29:11 NASB

My daughter, Cassie, like all teenagers, wondered about her future. She wrote to a friend:

> *I am just so thankful to God for everything*
> *He's done for me, as well as for others. Even when*
> *things are bad, He's stood next to me and things*
> *are a little less prone to becoming blown out of*
> *proportion by my emotions. . . . You know, I won-*
> *der what God is going to do with my life. Like my*
> *purpose. Some people become missionaries and*
> *things, but what about me? What does God have*
> *in store for me? For now, I'll just take it day by*
> *day. I'm confident that I'll know someday. Maybe*
> *I'll look back at my life and think, 'Oh, so that*
> *was it!' Isn't it amazing, this plan we're a part of?*

Little did my daughter know that her purpose would be to be martyred for her faith in the shootings at Columbine High School. As a result, millions have heard the gospel message.

Rejoice each day as you watch God's plan for you unfold. He does indeed have a plan for your life. These plans are for good and not for evil, to give you a future and a hope.

FAITH IN CRISIS

Polly McNabb,
editor

And we know that God causes all things to work together
for good to those who love God,
to those who are called according to His purpose.

ROMANS 8:28 NASB

How strong is our faith in a real crisis? I've had occasion to observe many examples through the years, but one stands out.

My friend's niece Susan was engaged to be married, and the wedding was just a week away. Susan's aunt Dorothy wondered if she were really ready for marriage. After all, she was only eighteen. Was she mature enough for all the responsibilities?

Then the call came. The groom-to-be was seriously injured in a motorcycle accident. In addition to other injuries, literally every bone in his face was broken, some crushed. How would an eighteen year old respond to such a crisis?

Aunt Dorothy's concerns were put to rest the moment she heard Susan's voice on the phone. "Oh, Aunt Dorothy," she exclaimed. "Guess what? God was preparing me for this accident even before it happened." And she explained that the night before, she had taken a whole roll of film, showing Curtis in every position, with close-ups of the face including front and side views. The doctors were able to blow up the photos and use them for reconstructing Curtis's face.

That is faith in the context of crisis!

CONFIDENCE

Michelle L. Pecanic,
teacher

*For the LORD will be your confidence
and will keep your foot from being snared.*
PROVERBS 3:26 NIV

I've always enjoyed school, which probably explains why I am now a teacher. But there was one part of school I avoided whenever possible—public speaking. I dreaded oral presentations so much, in fact, that I would become physically ill on the day of the presentation.

On one of these occasions, my mom shared the above Scripture with me. It took awhile for me to really believe it and claim God's promise for myself, but eventually I did. He provided confidence for me through many means. . . . He gave me encouraging friends and teachers and many opportunities for practice, including a speech class in college.

Eventually I got over the debilitating fear of public speaking and began to realize that the Lord is my confidence in every one of life's situations: sharing His love with others, following His will in my life, adapting to change, facing the unexpected. No matter what comes, He gives me confidence to face any situation with His strength.

What difficult situations are you facing today? Ask God for the confidence you need to overcome these difficulties.

FIVE WAYS TO MAKE YOUR DAY

Barbara Johnson,
Women of Faith speaker and writer

A joyful heart is good medicine.
PROVERBS 17:22 NASB

Give yourself a gift today: Be present with yourself. God is. Enjoy your own personality. God does.

You are going to make it through whatever is on your plate. You are not only a survivor; you are a winner. Here are five fun, sometimes foolish, always productive ways to put a smile on your face. Make your day!

1. Start a journal if you don't already have one. Write down five things you are thankful for today.
2. Think about this: If you were going to die tomorrow and were allowed to make only one phone call, who would you call and what would you say? Now, make that call.
3. Smile at yourself in the mirror. Wink back!
4. Hold all things loosely and mean it when you say, "Whatever, Lord!"
5. Find something to laugh about today. If all else fails, go get a joke book from the library, call the funniest person you know, or read this: What do you get when you cross an insomniac, an agnostic, and a dyslexic? Answer: A person who lies awake at night trying to decide if there really is a doG.

My Future

Angela Risley,
student,
Oklahoma Christian University

Commit your way to the LORD,
trust also in Him, and He will do it.

PSALM 37:5 NASB

Recently I've been having some serious doubts about my plans for the future and whether I am ready to take on life after graduation. While sharing these thoughts with a trusted friend, I was amazed at the wisdom she gave me. In the midst of my "I just don't know if I can do it" complaint, she looked at me and said something very powerful:

"In times like these, you have to listen to your fear. It's trying to tell you something very valuable, and you can't ignore it. You need to welcome it and let it teach you. Welcome it, but do not let it dictate how you live."

I certainly have never done that before. Just because of my young age, I realized that I was not allowing God to use me to my full potential, something great for His kingdom! I began to truly see what God was doing in my life and, in turn, became aware of what I was to do for Him. Now instead of being fearful about the future, I am looking forward to the future with excited anticipation of what God will do, and has been doing all along, as He directs my path.

HUMBLE FRIENDS

Kerry Stavert,
single parent of five

Humble yourselves in the sight of the Lord, and He will lift you up.
JAMES 4:10 NKJV

Theresa was the middle child in a family of eight, and so was her best friend, Linda. It seemed as though they had always known each other, and that was almost true, as they had spent many hours in the same playpen as babies. The greatest thing about their friendship was that it knew how to grow.

It started with Judy in fifth grade. Judy was considered "weird," but Theresa and Linda knew she at least deserved a friend. "How can you stand to watch her eat?" others would say. They refused to get drawn in. "Don't you think she has beautiful, thick hair?" they would counter. Judy didn't change her odd ways, but at least she was odd with two close friends.

By the time they got to high school, Theresa and Linda were eating lunch every day surrounded by an assortment of "misfits" like Judy. When Theresa was elected cheerleader, they were elated, and when Linda was crowned homecoming queen, there was not a dry eye among their friends.

Theresa and Linda were definitely beautiful girls. Their friends would tell you that was because they mirrored the beauty they saw in others.

THE ÉCLAIR INCIDENT

Beverly Plaugher,
writer

"Be sure your sin will find you out."
NUMBERS 32:23 NASB

É clair: an oblong cream puff with whipped cream or pudding filling.

Add chocolate to the top of an already wonderful éclair, and you have perfection—at least for me. A chocolate éclair could draw me into a bakery so fast that I could spin around and change directions on a dime.

In junior high school, I walked off campus many times at lunch break to go buy chocolate éclairs. I would devour each one as if I might never see another.

I was so into wanting "what I wanted" that I disobeyed the school rules and returned late to my class after lunch. I gave "wonderful" excuses to the teacher for my tardiness.

One very hot day after my excursion off campus, the principal kindly asked me to step into his office. I did. Mother was there. I was caught! The consequences were horrible, but I learned my lesson. I never saw another chocolate éclair for the remainder of the year. I stayed on campus, arrived to classes on time, and didn't tell lies to my teachers. To this day, I still love chocolate éclairs, but the memory of this sweet lesson still sends shivers down my spine.

WHO YOUR FRIENDS ARE SAYS A LOT ABOUT YOU

Kristi Norton,
teacher

> *He who walks with wise men will be wise,*
> *But the companion of fools will suffer harm.*
> PROVERBS 13:20 NASB

The adjustment from junior high to high school was dreadful. I was in a bigger school and not a single acquaintance landed in any of my classes. I was eager to befriend the first girl who said more than "hello." Unfortunately, that was the downfall of my freshman year. I tried to convince myself that even though my new friend was making poor choices, I was not. I even dared to say that my good example was a "witness" to her.

But when her threats against another student landed me in the principal's office, I realized that she was having more of an impact on me than I was on her. Thankfully, I wised up before she and her new companion were arrested for shoplifting over the summer.

Now my closest friends are those I fellowship with at church. We have a common purpose to love Christ and live a godly life. Most importantly, we are not afraid to hold each other accountable to truth and wise choices. A good friend is someone who encourages my relationship with God, not causes others to question it.

SURRENDER IS THE
BEGINNING OF PEACE

Deirdre Cantrell,
director of new believers ministry,
Saddleback Church

" 'Our Father who is in heaven...Your will be done,
On earth as it is in heaven.' "
MATTHEW 6:9–10 NASB

During the 90s, I spent a greater part of those years in a wheelchair and on crutches with an injury. I was told I might never walk normally again, but I could not accept that. So I struggled to get better, but I only seemed to get worse.

One day, I was sitting in my living room utterly exhausted and sobbing. I knew I could not live like this any longer. I needed to come to the point of accepting that I might never be healed and completely trust God with whatever happened.

So with tears in my eyes, I said to God, "It's okay if my life is different than what I had dreamed. I can accept this—as long as I know You are there." That prayer of surrender was the turning point of my life. I could accept whatever happened—because I knew He loved me.

If you are struggling with an unpleasant or painful circumstance and can't figure out why it's happening, do whatever you can to change it, but accept that God has a good plan no matter what happens. Learn to say, "It's okay, God." That's where the peace of surrender happens.

WRONG TURNS

Martha Bolton,
writer

We all stumble in many ways.
JAMES 3:2 NIV

If a car is inadvertently driven onto a field, does that make it a tractor? Of course not. It's still a car, even though it's being driven alongside a herd of cattle. (Sounds like my first driving test, but I digress.)

The driver would never say, "Oh, no, look what I've done! I made a wrong turn. Now, I've got a tractor instead of a car!"

That would be ridiculous, wouldn't it?

No matter where that car goes, it's still a car. If it ends up in a pond, it doesn't become a canoe or, depending on how deep the pond is, a submarine. It's a car. Even if you find catfish in the glove compartment, it's still a car. All the wrong turns in the world aren't going to change that fact.

Do you know that you are who you are too, no matter how many wrong turns you make? Wrong turns don't define you or alter your true identity. You have the same qualities you've always had. You're still valuable.

A car doesn't turn into a tractor by making a wrong turn, and a wrong turn doesn't change a person's worth either.

MOST IMPORTANT OF ALL

Gigi Graham Tchividjian,
writer and daughter of Billy Graham

"His master replied, 'Well done, good and faithful servant!
You have been faithful with a few things;
I will put you in charge of many things.
Come and share your master's happiness!' "

MATTHEW 25:21 NIV

We began class with a brief devotional. I must admit I was distracted by the singing of the birds, the warm breezes, and the sweet aromas. I found it hard to concentrate, until something my teacher said caught my attention.

"The only thing the Lord requires of us," she was saying, "is faithfulness."

I felt both excitement and peace at those words. There, sitting at my school desk, a huge weight was lifted from my shoulders. I had been feeling an awesome responsibility to "measure up." There was so much to live up to, so many big footsteps to walk in, so many examples to follow that I just didn't see how I was going to do it!

But if the Lord's only requirement of me was faithfulness, then He didn't expect me to be like anyone else! And if the importance was in my faithfulness and not in the "greatness" of my task, then with His help I could serve and please Him in my own unique way. What a comfort!

From that day on, my prayer was that no matter what He gave me to do—whether great or small, public or private, I would be faithful.

CASTING YOUR CARES ON GOD

Tabitha Neuenschwander,
editor of *Encounter* Magazine

> *Cast all your anxiety on him because he cares for you.*
> 1 PETER 5:7 NIV

The amount of things that race through our thoughts in one day is staggering:

- the opposite sex
- loneliness
- the pile of homework waiting for you at home
- your relationship (or lack of) with your parents
- what to wear at school
- what to do this coming weekend

It amazes me how much time we can spend thinking about everything but God, our Creator—the one who gave us the ability to think! When you are discouraged with the events of everyday life, remember a loving God whose arms are strong enough to hold all of your burdens, no matter how big you think they are. He wants to help you handle the ups and downs in life. God desires to one day look you in the face and say, "Well done, good and faithful servant!" (Matthew 25:21).

So when your mind is racing with thoughts about your future, whether it be what to wear to school or deciding if you want to obey your parents or not, consider how your decisions will affect your relationship with God. Will they separate you from Him or will they leave you standing in His presence?

THE GREED NEED

Martha Bolton,
writer

You have lived on earth in luxury and self-indulgence.
You have fattened yourselves in the day of slaughter.
JAMES 5:5 NIV

Do you know that you don't have to be rich to be a greedy person? Greedy people come with all sizes of bank accounts. In fact, greed has less to do with your net worth than with your attitude.

If people feel the world owes them something, that's greed. . .no matter how much or how little money they actually have. Maybe you've met some people like this. They complain about not having any money, but won't do anything to earn any. They sit and wait for success to fall into their laps. Success doesn't fall into laps. It's achieved by hard work and perseverance.

Greed can also be coveting. Instead of being happy about your friend's new dress, you have to have one just like it or better. That's coveting.

Greed can be manipulating people so they'll give you what you want. "If you don't let me borrow money to get that new CD, then you're not my friend."

There are plenty of other ways to exhibit greed, but they all come from self-centeredness, and we don't have to be rich to have that problem.

MAKING ROOM FOR GOD

Andrea Frankwitz,
associate professor of English,
Biola University

> *"Be still, and know that I am God;*
> *I will be exalted among the nations, I will be exalted in the earth."*
> *The LORD Almighty is with us; the God of Jacob is our fortress.*
>
> PSALM 46: 10–11 NIV

In our fast-paced world, it's easy to let our lives become saturated with numerous activities. We can find ourselves pulled in all different directions, whether it's school, work, church, or other interests. Some of us may even be tempted to measure the meaningfulness of our lives by how busy we are. If we're regularly attending church and involved in church activities, reading the Bible, and tithing, it's easy to trick ourselves into thinking we're close to God and pleasing Him with our service. Of course, as Christians, we want to partake of these activities. There is, however, a potential danger of being so busy that we actually crowd out God from our lives.

There is no substitute for being alone in God's presence. Even in our devotional time, we can be so busy reading His Word or making petition or giving praise that we forget just to be still. Being still in His presence means patiently waiting on God and listening to Him. As we are obedient in this call to be still, we cannot help but focus on our heavenly Father rather than ourselves. As we seek God in the stillness, we'll discover the joy of hearing His heartbeat.

THANKFULNESS IS A CHOICE

Deirdre Cantrell,
director of new believers ministry,
Saddleback Church

In everything give thanks;
for this is God's will for you in Christ Jesus.
1 THESSALONIANS 5:18 NASB

You would think every believer would automatically be thankful since we have so much to be thankful for. However, have you ever noticed that it is the complete opposite? We don't have to be reminded to complain about something, but we do have to be reminded to be thankful.

Thankfulness is a choice. Learning to be thankful in all things demonstrates our trust in God. We trust that, although we may not understand everything that is happening in our lives, we know that God is in complete control.

One way I have found to live in an atmosphere of thankfulness is to write down one thing I am thankful for each day. No matter how hard life may get, there is always something we can be thankful about. If nothing else, we can be thankful that God loves us and wants a personal relationship with us. Wait. . .think about that for a moment. The God of the whole universe, who is the creator of everything seen and unseen, wants to have fellowship with you! That is an awesome thought and definitely something for which to be thankful.

SACRIFICIAL GIVING

Mother Teresa,
Nobel Peace Prize winner

" 'You shall love your neighbor as yourself.' "
MATTHEW 22:39 NASB

We must grow in love and to do this we must go on loving. . .and giving until it hurts—the way Jesus did. Do ordinary things with extraordinary love: little things like caring for the sick and the homeless, the lonely and the unwanted, washing and cleaning for them.

You must give what will cost you something. . . . Then your gift becomes a sacrifice, which will have value before God. Any sacrifice is useful if done out of love.

Every day I see this love. . . . I was once walking down the street and a beggar came to me and he said, "Mother Teresa, everybody's giving to you, I also want to give to you. Today, for the whole day, I got only twenty-nine paise, and I want to give it to you." I thought for a moment: *If I take it, he will have nothing to eat tonight, and if I don't take it, I will hurt him.* So I put out my hands and I took the money. I have never seen such joy on anybody's face as I saw on his—that a beggar, he too, could give to Mother Teresa.

FREE TO CRY

Barbara Johnson,
Women of Faith speaker

Those who sow in tears shall reap with joyful shouting.
PSALM 126:5 NASB

You don't have to grin and bear it. You don't have to be holier-than-thou, keeping up a "spiritual" front. . . . Tears are God's gift to His precious children. When we cry, we allow our bodies to function according to God's design—and we embrace one of the "perks" He offers to relieve our stress.

Someone said, "God will accept a broken heart, but He must have all the pieces." As He stitches those pieces back together, the moisture of tears softens and makes flexible His strong thread of healing in our lives. Big wet tears are part of the rich human experience.

. . . Do you realize what a gift it is to feel, even if it hurts?

. . . Sometimes allowing yourself to cry is the scariest thing you'll ever do. And the bravest. It takes a lot of courage to face the facts, stare loss in the face, bare your heart, and let it bleed. But it is the only way to cleanse your wounds and prepare them for healing. God will take care of the rest.

BETTER THAN A FAIRY TALE

Natalie Lloyd,
writer and *Brio* columnist

The mind of man plans his way, but the LORD directs his steps.
PROVERBS 16:9 NASB

If you've blown it and gotten deeper into a relationship than you should have, that doesn't mean your relationship with God can't be restored. We are never, ever worthless. No matter what's happened, no matter that we might have called something "love" to try to justify a relationship, we can't be separated from the love of God. Don't let what happened in the past make you think you're no good. That's a huge lie. God is love, and He's waiting and ready to offer forgiveness and see you as totally clean and holy.

God's plan is a lot better than any fairy tale! Before we can ever even think of getting serious in another relationship, the one with Him has to be the most important one we'll ever have. God is using this time to create in us some amazing qualities. He knows the exact timing and the unique way He's going to place someone in our lives. Be patient—he'll be worth waiting for!

THE PIANO RECITAL

June Hetzel,
education professor,
Biola University

Pride goes before destruction,
and a haughty spirit before stumbling.
PROVERBS 16:18 NASB

Pleased and proud of my long red dress and first pair of heels, I proudly pranced to the platform, where I smoothly played "Autumn Leaves." Applause rang out as I glided off the piano bench, making my way back across the platform, heels clicking triumphantly. As I neared the edge of the platform, a tuxedoed young man held out his hand to assist me as I "stepped" off the platform. Unfortunately, one of my lovely new heels hooked the edge of the platform, and I tumbled badly. So much for fancy-wancy new heels, and thank God for tuxedoed young men. I was as red as my dress when I finally located my seat and thought of nothing other than the tumble for the remainder of the recital.

Much of life is like this piano recital. The Lord gives us gifts and talents, and He expects a peak performance. Unfortunately, we sometimes get so full of ourselves that we become prideful and take a bad spill. Luckily for us, He loves us no matter what and is there to pick up the pieces. Our job is to stop thinking about ourselves and to focus on serving Him with our gifts.

ENCOURAGING OTHERS

Diane Guido,
associate dean,
Azusa Pacific University

Therefore, encourage one another and build each other up,
just as in fact you are doing.
1 THESSALONIANS 5:11 NIV

I was generally an upbeat and content teenager, but I had a long face one spring morning during a class break. Mr. Nelson, a supportive school counselor, approached me and asked what was wrong. I didn't mind sharing with him that my boyfriend and I had just broken up. I was definitely feeling low.

But just when sadness seemed so unavoidable, Mr. Nelson talked to me about thinking optimistically and about being hopeful. "Be strong," he said. "Don't let this situation get you down; you can make a bright future for yourself." He challenged me to dwell on the positive things in my life, to be a pleasant person, and to work for and to expect only the best. His spirit of encouragement spoke to my heart, and he truly cheered me up.

Mr. Nelson taught me that morning not only to challenge myself to be hopeful in down times, but he also taught me the importance of encouraging others. Even today, years later, his words are encouraging, and I now look for opportunities to help others as he helped me. A few kind words spoken with heartfelt compassion can truly make a difference in others' lives.

AN ART LESSON

Joni Eareckson Tada,
quadriplegic writer and speaker

*But we all, with unveiled face, beholding as in a mirror the glory
of the Lord, are being transformed into the same image
from glory to glory, just as from the Lord, the Spirit.*

2 CORINTHIANS 3:18 NASB

When I'm at my art easel, secondhand information won't do. If I'm working on a painting of daisies, I must have a vase of fresh daisies to study. There's no way that a photograph can convey the dark tones of real shadows or the thin transparency of a petal.

When I fail to study the real thing, my paintings show it. They lack life if I've only worked from photographs or other people's ideas. And what is true for the artist is true for the Christian. So many believers settle for secondhand information as they seek to know the Lord better. Some only get to know the Lord through other people. They feel energy from a friend's testimony and then attempt to transfer another's experience into their life. It won't work.

If a painting is to shine with life, it must represent the real thing. If a Christian is to shine with the light of Jesus, it will mean taking time to get close to the real thing or, in this case, the real Person. The closer we draw to Him, the more our life will look, feel, and be. . .real.

HOLINESS

Rebecca Manley Pippert,
writer

> " 'I am the LORD your God; consecrate yourselves and be holy,
> because I am holy.' "
>
> LEVITICUS 11:44 NIV

What is the fruit of a life submitted to God? We become like Him! One of God's goals is to shape our character so that we will manifest His kindness, mercy, love, purity, wisdom, and so on in ways that are reflected through our own distinctive personalities. To put it another way, God is making us holy.

But there is a requirement in learning how to submit to God's authority: humility. We won't get very far in the development of holiness if we are defensive about our flaws. That is why truly holy people are so easy to be with. They have been around God too long to try to pretend they are perfect. They are the first to acknowledge their pride and their faults.

Then why are holy people so joyful and radiant? One reason is that they know the answer to their character problem doesn't reside in them but with God. They don't try to please God through the efforts of the flesh, such as moralism and legalism, but by their obedient walk in the Spirit. They know a surrendered life comes by listening to God, walking in step with Him.

MOVIN' ON

Jennifer Knapp,
recording artist

Trust in the LORD with all your heart
and lean not on your own understanding;
in all your ways acknowledge him,
and he will make your paths straight.
PROVERBS 3:5–6 NIV

When I first became a Christian, one of my strong tendencies in life was to worry about and linger in my past. The idea of someone, like God, being faithful to forgive and forget was totally new to me—and somewhat unbelievable.

Since then, I've learned that worrying about something that has already been done and that I cannot control is what I call a real "ET" (energy taker) in life. Why should I waste energy on the past that could be used much better on the future?

When I finally got it and trusted what God says in the Bible, my burdens became lessened—I was set free. That belief and trust in God's forgiveness allowed me to pursue my God-given passions and take off on my dreams!

By reading the Bible, listening to God's voice, and then believing what He says, my true passions have been revealed and developed.

BEAUTY IS MORE THAN SKIN DEEP

Deirdre Cantrell,
director of new believers ministry,
Saddleback Church

How many are your works, O LORD!
In wisdom you made them all.
PSALM 104:24 NIV

Ever have one of those days when you feel just plain ugly? You look in the mirror trying to see something that just doesn't seem to be there. Well, I have been having one of those days for over a year now. . . . I always heard about your beauty going when you got older (not that I was a raving beauty to begin with). It is at times like these that I run to God for His perspective on what beauty really is.

Do you honestly know how God sees you? He sees you as a beautiful bride adorned for her wedding day. He sees you as His child who takes after His beauty and design. He sees you as a precious stone, apple of His eye, and someone whom He gave His life for.

We live in a society where people see beauty as only "skin deep." God looks past the skin right into your heart. . .that is where the true beauty is. Don't let the world deceive you into its mold of what beauty is. Look to God and believe Him for what is truly beautiful. . .you!

BROKEN BUT NOT
DESTROYED

Nancy C. Anderson,
conference and retreat speaker

For He Himself has said,
"I will never leave you nor forsake you."
HEBREWS 13:5 NKJV

I paced the floor of the high school cafeteria as I waited for my boyfriend, John. He was late for lunch, so I went looking for him. As I walked around the corner, near the science lab, I saw him. He was walking, hand in hand, with my best friend, Brenda!

She had the decency to turn her head in shame, but he looked me in the eye, smiled a cruel smile, and casually said, "Hi, Nance." They kept walking. I fell against the wall as my knees and heart folded.

He had been my whole world. That day, I thought my life was over, and I felt less than worthless. He broke my heart and my spirit. But I learned a valuable lesson as I watched him, a month later, break Brenda's heart too.

I never again measured my worth by another person's loyalty. As I learned to lean on the Lord, I saw that God's love for me is consistent and unfailing and that I am very valuable to Him. People may disappoint me, but He will never leave me or betray me.

He Understands and Enables

Anna Y. Wong,
early childhood director,
Sea Ridge Community Church

And the deeds of a man's hands will return to him.
PROVERBS 12:14 NASB

During my freshman year at Biola University, I began the year with excitement and zest. What a tremendous blessing it was to be taught, led, and challenged by Christian professors! What fun it was to meet new friends from all over the world!

Homework, however, required many hours of my days and nights. Exams, assignments, and textbook reading came like an unrelenting tidal wave. When I came upon Ecclesiastes 12:12, I felt God totally understood my moments of weariness. What a comfort. I asked Him for the strength to accomplish all that I had to complete. As I sought to honor Him with my efforts, I was able to experience His empowering. Semester by semester, He faithfully enabled me. After four years of hard work, I was jubilant as I marched up the commencement aisle.

Thank You, Lord, especially for Your great understanding and faithful enabling!

SCARED

Jeanetta Sims,
instructor,
Oklahoma Christian University

I will lie down and sleep in peace,
for you alone, O LORD, make me dwell in safety.

PSALM 4:8 NIV

After months of prayerfully waiting on the results of my application, the words of my high school teacher confirmed God's response—I was selected for an eight-week, exchange student scholarship to Japan.

Throughout my junior year, I raised funds for the summer trip, solicited gifts for my host family, and completed paperwork for my passport—all in preparation to leave. Finally, at the airport with tearful good-byes to my family and friends, I was off to meet my new host family and experience life as a student in Japan.

The first night nestled in my new Tokyo home, a wave of panic hit me. I was living in a different country, trying to learn a new culture, working to decipher a difficult language, and at the total disposal of people I knew nothing about. God had blessed me with the experience I had asked of Him. Now, thousands of miles from home, my excitement had faded, and I was scared. That night, I realized my total dependence on God.

I missed home occasionally, but throughout my stay in Japan, I slept peacefully knowing that wherever God has blessed me to be, He is able to secure my safety.

FRIENDS FIRST

Beverly Plaugher,
writer

> *"You will know them by their fruits."*
> MATTHEW 7:16 NASB

Perfection is not possible when it comes to selecting boyfriends and husbands. However, go for as close to perfection as possible, and try to be friends first. The following qualifications might be close to perfection, but there is no guarantee: 1) A Christian who attends church and reads the Bible; 2) Honest—trustworthy; 3) Tender and loves children; 4) Considerate to everyone; 5) Respectful of his parents; 6) Good sense of humor; 7) Saves money but knows when to spend it; 8) Owns up to his mistakes—does not blame others.

Observe the behavior of the guy you like. Examine the fruit in his life. Pray for God's will. Try to be friends first and delay a dating relationship.

When I was twelve years old, there was a guy named Richard who was the cutest guy in church and had the qualities listed above. I prayed and prayed and asked the Lord if I could marry him. Richard and I were friends for a long time first before we ever started dating. Then, we started dating when I was sixteen, and when I was twenty years old, he became my husband!

Ask Not What Your Church Can Do for You, but What You Can Do for Your Church

Kristi Norton,
teacher

*And let us consider how to stimulate
one another to love and good deeds,
not forsaking our own assembling together.*

HEBREWS 10:24–25 NASB

The last thing I wanted to do on the weekend was wake up early for church. Mother worked at the church, so it became my duty to be in attendance for all three services. As a teenager, just one service was long enough, and lucky me got to sit through three of them. After six months of this routine, I started to wonder about what else I could be doing with my time. I discovered a need for Sunday school teachers for the four and five year olds and was pleasantly surprised when they let me teach a class. I finally found something to look forward to.

I still enjoy teaching in the church. Getting involved in ministry has made going to church fun and exciting. I look forward to every Sunday and Wednesday. Most importantly, what was once a search for a cure to boredom has now turned into a passion. I now see how God was preparing me to become a teacher even at the young age of thirteen.

BEAUTY IS SOUL DEEP

USE THE MOMENTUM

Barbara Johnson,
Women of Faith speaker and writer

> *But you will receive power*
> *when the Holy Spirit has come upon you.*
> ACTS 1:8 NASB

When I learned to ride a bicycle, I did it badly—at least in comparison to other neighborhood kids. I had no sense of balance. I'd wobble and roll, wibble and rock. I ended up with scraped knees and shins. It seemed no matter how much I wanted to, I couldn't get the two-wheeler to stay upright. I thought I'd be the only kid in second grade who couldn't ride a bike.

Fortunately, a neighborhood friend offered to teach me how to ride. He seemed so confident. "It's simple," he said. "The problem is you haven't got enough momentum going to keep in balance. Once you get going fast enough long enough, you won't have any trouble at all."

Someone said, "Our glory is not in never falling, but in rising each time we fall." I believe the secret of success is to stay cool and calm on top and pedal like crazy underneath. When you do fall and skin your knees, get up again and start all over under the impetus of the Holy Spirit. Stay in the race. Find your pace, then shift into cruise gear. Use the momentum!

CONFIDENCE IN CHRIST

Debrah Jay Smith,
Young Life area director,
Huntington Beach, California

*Whatever I have, wherever I am, I can make it
through anything in the One who makes me who I am.*
PHILIPPIANS 4:13 THE MESSAGE

As a young girl, I filled countless hours playing just beyond where the sidewalk ends—in the gutter! Day after day my twin sister and I would report to the gutter for "toothpick races." It was a game we created to chase away summer boredom and to launch ourselves into an imaginary world. With enthusiasm and expectancy, we would place toothpicks side by side in the overflowing gutter and reluctantly release them to that unpredictable "war zone" beneath our feet.

The toothpick's journey was always a slow and risky one. There was, after all, a web of intimidating obstacles along the journey. Overgrown weeds creeping through cement cracks would undoubtedly stall them. The toothpicks often got lodged in a wad of discarded bubble gum or lost in a heap of neglected trash. The toothpicks eventually emerged dented, damaged, or broken by the trek.

It was a childhood game. But it is also a description of my teenage years. So many days my splintered life drifted through dangerous obstacles. Peer pressure was great, and I was constantly tempted. But I had a confidence in Christ that allowed me to navigate anything. His strength sustained me on a treacherous voyage.

LIVING SACRIFICE

Carla Perez,
living sacrifice

Therefore I urge you, brethren, by the mercies of God,
to present your bodies a living and holy sacrifice,
acceptable to God, which is your spiritual service of worship.

ROMANS 12:1 NASB

I had taken a vacation with my aunts to Canada. One afternoon we stood on the Canadian side of Niagara Falls, gazing as millions of gallons of water surged over the precipice. I was amazed to notice a small boat, The Maid of the Mist, at the foot of the roaring falls. It inched closer to the roaring water. The tour boat, which ferries passengers in for the breathtakingly close view of the falls, borrowed its name from the young American Indian maidens, "maids of the mist." One maiden was chosen each year to board a small canoe and heroically ride over the tumbling waters, sacrificing her life for the future peace and prosperity of the tribe.

Thankfully, God does not ask me to drift over a fall to my destruction. However, God does ask me, like the maids of the mist, to be a sacrifice—but He wants me alive. He wants me to be His living sacrifice, using my gifts and talents to glorify Him and to love others.

Lord, I give You everything I have. Help me love others and glorify Your name.

JESUS, I JUST WANTED TO BE SURE OF YOU

Kathy Troccoli,
recording artist and writer

"I will never leave you nor forsake you."
JOSHUA 1:5 NIV

I love to haunt old bookstores, antique shops, floral stores, and quaint little restaurants with a section of one-of-a-kind cards. I remember the day I picked up one that showed Winnie-the-Pooh and Piglet on the front, walking hand in hand. Their conversation went like this:

"Pooh?" Piglet said.

"Yes, Piglet."

"Oh, nothing. I just wanted to be sure of you."

I stared at it awhile, smiled, and then read it a few more times. I've asked this question of close friends at many different times in my life, in many different ways. I need the safety, the reassurance, the knowing they are right there and that I am loved.

So often my daily experiences remind me of my relationship with Jesus. The simplicity of that exchange between Pooh and Piglet mirrors an almost daily conversation between God and myself:

"Jesus?" I say.

"Yes, Kathy."

"Oh, nothing, I just wanted to be sure of You."

The mention of His name. My protector. My deliverer. My Lord. My comfort. My reason for being. If I can be sure of anything, I can be sure of Him.

PRESSING ON

Jane Carr,
Christian education professor,
Biola University

> *But one thing I do: forgetting what lies behind*
> *and reaching forward to what lies ahead,*
> *I press on toward the goal for the prize*
> *of the upward call of God in Christ Jesus.*
>
> PHILIPPIANS 3:13–14 NASB

In March I set out to do something I had wanted to do all my life: run the Los Angeles Marathon.

The miles went by quickly at first, and then it happened. . .mile 22. . .mile 22. . . . The miles seemed to get farther and farther apart. At mile 23, I distinctly remember thinking, "I want to quit." Now I know that it seems strange to think of quitting when you are just 3.2 miles from the finish line, but it happens. The enthusiasm you first had begins to fade; fatigue and even boredom set in.

The Christian life is a lot like a marathon. It is a journey not a destination. It is a process of growth, not instant perfection. It takes daily conscious decisions to follow Christ regardless of how you feel. Every time a runner looks back over her shoulder, she loses precious seconds in a race. As Christians, we must leave our past failures behind us and allow God's merciful grace to cover us.

Well, despite mile 23, I didn't quit, and I have a nice gold finishers' medal to prove it. You can too, if you'll just press on.

MY PLANS OR GOD'S PLANS?

Joy Mosbarger,
college professor

If I rise on the wings of the dawn, if I settle on the far side
of the sea, even there your hand will guide me,
your right hand will hold me fast.
PSALM 139:9–10 NIV

Recently a friend and I had plans to go to a movie. She got delayed in traffic and didn't arrive until half an hour after the movie had started. I admit that I don't like it when my plans are thwarted. I tend to live as if I have control over the events of my life. But every so often the Lord shatters that illusion and reminds me that the events of my life are out of my control. He leads the way and directs my steps. Often His path is one I would never choose on my own, full of unexpected twists and turns and unanticipated potholes and obstacles. My plans tend to be predictable and safe; His plans are surprising and scary. But His way can lead to adventure and joy that I never would have encountered on my own.

My friend and I missed that movie I'd wanted to see. But instead we enjoyed some great fellowship over some pie. Our conversation refreshed and encouraged me in much deeper ways than a movie could have. God really does know what He's doing. I'm so much better off when I just trust Him and delight in the journey, wherever it takes me.

In the Yuck of Life

Shelly Cunningham,
Christian education professor,
Biola University

Praise be to the God and Father of our Lord Jesus Christ,
the Father of compassion and the God of all comfort,
who comforts us in all our troubles,
so that we can comfort those in any trouble with
the comfort we ourselves have received from God.

2 CORINTHIANS 1:3-4 NIV

Is your heart ever so heavy you feel like you can't move? You want to stay in bed with the blanket over your head and hope all your problems go away. They don't. When you crawl out of bed, the problems are still there.

You are not left alone to carry a heavy heart by yourself. The God who loves you and sees you and knows your name is called the "Father of compassion and the God of all comfort." It is a promise of the Bible that this God "comforts us in all our troubles." He walks right through the dirt and darkness and the yuck of life with us.

I once heard it said that God has our picture on His refrigerator. When your heart hurts, He opens His arms of comfort to draw you in and hold you close while you are in the middle of the yuck.

A FEAST FOR SINNERS

Sheila Walsh,
writer and recording artist

"But the tax collector stood at a distance.
He would not even look up to heaven,
but beat his breast and said,
'God, have mercy on me, a sinner!'
I tell you that this man, rather than the other,
went home justified before God.
For everyone who exalts himself will be humbled,
and he who humbles himself will be exalted."

LUKE 18:13–14 NIV

One Sunday evening in London, the Archbishop of Canterbury was delivering a sermon at Westminster Chapel. At the end of the message, all who believed in Christ Jesus were invited to come up to the altar and partake of communion.

The Archbishop noticed that the only one who did not come to the rail was a shabby-looking man who sat in the last row of the church, hiding in the dim light. The clergyman carried the elements of bread and wine to this man and asked him if he knew Christ as his Savior. The man said he did.

"Then take and eat, my son," he said.

"I'm not worthy, sir."

"Then this feast is for you," he replied. "This is a feast for sinners."

God's grace provides a Lamb for sin and a feast for sinners.

BEAUTY IS SOUL DEEP

YOU WHAT?!

Martha Bolton,
writer

*Just then his disciples returned and were surprised
to find him talking with a woman.*
JOHN 4:27 NIV

Do you realize that when someone asks if he or she can confide in us, and we agree, we're not only promising to keep that person's confidence, but we're also assuring him or her that our friendship isn't going to change after hearing it?

When friends tell us what's on their hearts, it's because they're trusting us to still be their friends afterward. They don't expect, nor do they deserve, to receive a cold shoulder or unreturned telephone calls because now that we know the things they "struggle with," they're not really the kind of friend we want to have hanging around.

Don't get me wrong. There certainly are dangers in having negative influences in your life. Jesus warns us of that. But being a friend to someone preconfession and ignoring him or her postconfession doesn't seem very Christian, does it? Jesus saw the sins of the woman at the well, yet He still was a friend to her. He's our example. We're supposed to act like Him.

If a friend opens up to you, it's because there's something about you that makes him or her feel safe. Your friend feels you can be trusted with his or her faults. Don't prove your friend wrong by disappearing after he or she confesses them.

THE GIFT OF SERVICE

Joni Eareckson Tada,
quadriplegic writer and speaker

*This service that you perform is not only supplying the needs
of God's people but is also overflowing in many expressions of
thanks to God. Because of the service by which you have
proved yourselves, men will praise God for the obedience
that accompanies your confession of the gospel of Christ,
and for your generosity in sharing with them and with everyone else.*

2 CORINTHIANS 9:12–13 NIV

O ccasionally, the blues weigh us down. And I'm no exception. The other day I was struggling all morning to breathe comfortably. I'd only been sitting in my wheelchair a few hours, and my back ached miserably. I couldn't concentrate. I just wanted to go back to bed and forget the day.

That happened to be the morning I received a note of encouragement from the eleven-year-old daughter of a friend. Her words? "I want you to know, Joni, that I appreciate your life. You've really helped me overcome a lot of things. Thanks for loving God, and I hope you continue to serve Him with all your heart."

Just a simple letter with a few bright words. But God used that scrawled note to bring sharply into focus the enormous value of serving others in love. Only the other side of eternity will reveal to you and me the immense value our small sacrifices of service have accomplished.

JOY IN TRIALS

Brittany Waggoner,
college student and writer

Consider it pure joy, my brothers,
whenever you face trials of many kinds, because you know
that the testing of your faith develops perseverance.
Perseverance must finish its work, so that you may be mature
and complete, not lacking anything.

JAMES 1:2–4 NIV

It is a human response to ask "Why?" when bad things happen. If you have ever spent time baby-sitting, you know that no matter what you tell the children to do, they always ask, "Why?" We may not be children, but our response is the same when we are disappointed. Our response is even more emphatic when we face devastating disappointments or several disappointments at the same time.

The book of James gives us some insight into the question, "Why?" Notice, we are to "consider" these trials to be a "joy." Say what? I don't know about you, but the trials I go through are not a party! This is precisely why the Scripture doesn't say, "it will be joyful to go through trials." Instead, it says that we should "consider," or look upon, our trials as a good thing. The key is our attitude, not the circumstances. That is the one thing we can change.

What is the key to changing our attitude? It is the assurance of what trials produce in our life. This is the process God is using to produce something of value— endurance—in our lives.

EVE MADE ME DO IT

Lorraine Peterson,
writer

"The soul who sins is the one who will die.
The son will not share the guilt of the father,
nor will the father share the guilt of the son.
The righteousness of the righteous man will be credited to him,
and the wickedness of the wicked will be charged against him."

 EZEKIEL 18:20 NIV

I walked into the principal's office just in time to hear, "But he started it!" cut off by the principal's booming voice: "I don't care what the other guy did. I want to know what you did." Just as the student had to face the principal because of his own actions, each of us must face God, knowing that we are responsible for our own deeds; we can't blame anybody else.

My father tells about the first lie he ever heard my sister tell: "Chickie did it. Don't spank me." She was barely two. No one has to teach us to cover up for our mistakes and sins. That comes naturally. If we don't stop blaming other people, we will never build an honest and healthy relationship with God.

One of the devil's best tricks to keep us from having pure hearts is getting us to concentrate on the faults and sins of others. If God had a loudspeaker in the sky to give us constant audible advice, I think we'd often hear, "Mind your own business." Confess your sin without blaming anyone but yourself.

"YES, LORD!"

Debbie Graham,
writer

*"I am the vine; you are the branches. . .
apart from me you can do nothing."*

JOHN 15:5 NIV

T his is how I want to feel all the time," Karin
    thought—peaceful, joyful, and expectant about
life. Having been invited to the Bible study by a friend,
Karin was captivated by the presence of Jesus.

Karin's feelings of well-being lasted only as long
as she was in her Christian environment. Karin's daily
life seemed to overwhelm her. She would cry out,
"Lord, why aren't You helping me?" or "Why is my life
so hard and other people seem to be sailing through
their lives?" Karin decided obedience was the answer.
She mustered all her will to walk in Jesus' ways so He
would bless her. She failed, became exhausted, and
wondered if she could live the Christian life.

One day God's glory came to Karin in prayer.
"Will you be Mine?" Jesus asked. Only then did Karin
understand that Jesus wanted her to belong only to
Him, that Jesus was personally inviting her to be part
of His family, that Jesus was her only source. She finally
understood that Jesus was in control of her daily existence and that He held her soul and her life in His
loving hands. Jesus' presence, beauty, tenderness, and
assurance caused her to cry, "Yes, Lord!"

In the Desert
but not Deserted

Gigi Graham Tchividjian,
writer and daughter of Billy Graham

Praise be to the God and Father of our Lord Jesus Christ!
In his great mercy he has given us new birth
into a living hope through the resurrection of
Jesus Christ from the dead.

1 PETER 1:3 NIV

Sometimes I just don't feel spiritual. I don't feel like praying. I have little or no desire to read my Bible. I become concerned. If I were truly in love with Jesus, wouldn't I feel it and want to spend as much time with Him as possible?

Often it is in times like these that I find I need the Lord the most. When I feel like reading my Bible and praying, I probably don't need it as much as when I don't feel it. I also try to find small springs of water: a devotional book of encouraging words, a verse to meditate upon, a quiet walk when I can talk to the Lord, honestly expressing myself—after all, He knows all about me anyway. It's so wonderful just to be able to be myself with Him.

During my desert time, I try not to sit around lamenting my lack of feelings, nor do I try to arouse my feelings. I simply wait in faith.

In my desert, I have come to accept my position in Christ as sure and secure, because it has nothing to do with me and everything to do with Him.

LETTING GOD SET YOUR AGENDA

Lavonna Martin-Floreal,
Olympic athlete and 100-meter-hurdle silver medalist,
with Dave Branon

The mind of man plans his way,
But the LORD directs his steps.

PROVERBS 16:9 NASB

As late as the fall of 1997, [Lavonna] was still struggling with letting go of her track career. "I know that God is saying to Me, 'I'm your source. I'm your source for everything.' Not long ago, I was still making track my source.

"I was reading in the book *Experiencing God*, and I felt God was asking me, 'When are you going to yield to me? When are you going to trust Me?'

"I finally said, 'I'm done, Lord. If You want me to keep working at Target [which she was doing at the time] in order to get me where You want me to be, then I'll just yield.' "

For an athlete who has reached the highest level of success, it's not easy to be willing to stay out of the spotlight and to give up the glamour associated with world-class sports. But if Lavonna Martin-Floreal has learned anything, she has learned that God has plenty more surprises for her as she uses her silver medal status as a witness for Him. "God knows what He is doing," she says.

DESIGNER ORIGINAL

Tonya Ruiz,
author of *Beauty Quest—A Model's Journey*

For you formed my inward parts:
You covered me in my mother's womb.
I will praise You, for I am fearfully and wonderfully made;
Marvelous are Your works, and that my soul knows very well.

PSALM 139:13–14 NKJV

I was living in New York and working as a fashion model. One morning the agency sent me on an interview. When I entered the photographer's studio, I saw some of the most gorgeous girls in the world, and I realized that all my hopes and dreams of becoming rich and famous depended on me looking better than them. I sat down next to a famous model, who had dark blond hair, piercing blue-green eyes, and high-chiseled cheekbones. She was so exquisite that I wanted to die, or at least be invisible, so I could sneak out and go hate myself in solitude. I wondered, *Why couldn't I look more like her?*

As a teenager, I was never happy being myself. I always wanted to look like someone else. Since then, I have learned that I am God's artwork, a unique, one-of-a-kind masterpiece. Famous fashion designers label all their creations; even Barbie has Mattel stamped on her back. God created me and I wear His label, "Fashioned by God, a Designer Original."

Marvelous Plans

June Hetzel,
education professor,
Biola University

O Lord, you are my God; I will exalt you and praise your name,
for in perfect faithfulness you have done marvelous things,
things planned long ago.

Isaiah 25:1 niv

The Israelites were blessed by God. While wandering in the wilderness, God sent bread from heaven each morning in the form of manna. When the people complained they had no meat, God sent quail. When the people complained they had no water, God gave water from a rock.

It was amazing—everything the people needed, God provided in the wilderness over and over again. Yet, when the Israelites came to the Promised Land, only Joshua and Caleb believed God would help them conquer the land. Everyone else was afraid and complained—again. Because of their faith, Joshua and Caleb were the only ones from their generation that God allowed to move into the Promised Land.

Do you keep doubting God? Did you know God loves you and has a marvelous plan for your life that He planned long ago? That wonderful plan is His promised land for you. Trust Him to be faithful. Exalt and praise His name, even when you have to wait for these wonderful plans to unfold.

READY FOR HEAVEN

Misty Bernall,
mother of teen martyr Cassie Bernall

*For the Lord Himself will descend from heaven with a shout,
with the voice of the archangel and with the trumpet of God,
and the dead in Christ will rise first. Then we who are alive and
remain shall be caught up together with them in the clouds to
meet the Lord in the air, and so we shall always be with the Lord.*

1 THESSALONIANS 4:16–17 NASB

I buried my daughter after she was killed at Columbine High School for standing up for her faith. Jordan, a friend of Cassie's, recalls her thoughts at Cassie's funeral:

> *I've begun to think about how temporary everything is, including human life. Seeing that coffin go into the ground at the burial and knowing that it's all going to return to dust—that really got me thinking. All of a sudden my car, my apartment, my money, my material things, and even school didn't seem so important anymore. I took a week off from college because it was more important for me to be with my friends and everyone at church. Not necessarily to talk, but just to be together and appreciate them.*

I think a death like this should shake us and wake us up. It should get us asking, "What is important in life?" To me, the [most] important thing is that she was prepared to go at a moment's notice.

TILL DEATH US DO PART

Lorraine Peterson,
writer

> "Suppose one of you wants to build a tower.
> Will he not first sit down and estimate the cost to see
> if he has enough money to complete it?"
>
> LUKE 14:28 NIV

If you've ever attended a traditional wedding cere-mony, you've heard things like, "For better, for worse; for richer, for poorer; in sickness and in health. . .till death do us part." Taken seriously, that's a tremendous commitment to live up to. Would you describe your relationship with Jesus Christ as that kind of commitment, or do you think of it as "Try Jesus for ninety days; there's nothing to lose, and there's a money-back guarantee"?

There are facts you base your life on—an opera-tion will cure appendicitis, it's safer to slow down when driving around mountain curves, and jumping from a twelfth-story window is hazardous to your health. Whether or not you feel like acting in accordance with these facts, they are valid. They are true whether or not you understand the reasons behind them and whether or not everyone else believes in them.

You must commit yourself to Jesus because of the facts—He is "the way, the truth, and the life"—and not because He'll give you a new high. Following Jesus and His truth has great end results, but it takes a life-time commitment.

TAKE THE PLUNGE!

Sheila Walsh,
writer and recording artist

*Then he said to them all: "If anyone would come
after me, he must deny himself and take up
his cross daily and follow me."*

LUKE 9:23 NIV

I didn't learn to swim until I was sixteen years old. I knew how to do it in theory; I was just too afraid to take the plunge.

One day, I decided that this was the day. I went to the swimming pool by the beach and jumped off the diving board into the deep end. There was nothing gracious about my performance, but I swam. I was terrified and thrilled and alive!

In *Mere Christianity*, C. S. Lewis writes, "If you want joy, power, peace, eternal life, you must get close to or even into the thing that has them." In other words, you must take the plunge! God is not a stagnant pool but a mighty river running faster and faster, suddenly curving in a different direction, resting awhile, then racing off again in breathtaking power and beauty. There is no greater adventure (for someone) than throwing everything they have in with God, without reservation.

How sad it would be to stand on the edge of the water of life and never get wet. Jump in! The Most High will be there, and you will be terrified and thrilled and alive!

THE ADVICE COLUMN

Mabel Hale,
writer

"My Father will honor the one who serves me."
JOHN 12:26 NIV

Sometimes, much to my amusement, I read in the magazines those comical letters that girls write to the beauty specialists. If these letters could all be put together into one, it would read something like this: "How am I to make myself pretty so that I shall be admired for my good looks? I want to be rid of all my blemishes, my freckles and pug nose and pimples and stringy hair. Tell me, Miss Specialist, how to make myself beautiful."

Every girl longs to be beautiful. There is in woman a nature as deep as humanity that compels her to strive for good looks.

A desire to be beautiful is not unwomanly. But, mark you, true beauty is not of the face but of the soul. There is a beauty so deep and lasting that it will shine out of the homeliest face and make it comely. This is the beauty to be first sought and admired. It is a quality of the mind and heart and is manifested in word and deed. A happy heart, a smiling face, loving words and deeds, and a desire to be of service will make any girl beautiful.

DEAR READER,

If this book has brought up an issue for which you need help (e.g., depression, peer pressure, uncertainty of salvation, low self-esteem, dating problems, an eating disorder, etc.), we encourage you to talk immediately with a trustworthy adult who has a strong relationship with the Lord—your mom or dad, a neighbor, a teacher, a school counselor, a health professional, or a counselor. Remember, you are not alone, and God did not design for you to be alone in your struggles. God designed you to live in community with His people to fulfill the beautiful life He desires for you.

If this book has meant a lot to you, we'd love to hear from you. Write us at:

Barbour Publishing, Inc.
attn: June Hetzel, Ph.D. and Michelle Lee, Ph.D.
Beauty Is Soul Deep Editors
P.O. Box 719
Uhrichsville, Ohio 44683

May God's blessing be upon you and may your beauty be "soul deep" through the transforming work of the Holy Spirit.

With love,
JUNE AND MICHELLE

ACKNOWLEDGMENTS

Barbour Publishing, Inc., expresses its appreciation to all those who generously gave permission to reprint and/or adapt copyrighted material. Diligent effort has been made to identify, locate, and contact copyright holders and to secure permission to use copyrighted material. If any permissions or acknowledgments have been inadvertently omitted or if such permissions were not received by the time of publication, the publisher would sincerely appreciate receiving complete information so that correct credit can be given in future editions.

"Beyond Comparison," "Face Your Fear," "Beauty and the Feast Beast," "Broken But Not Destroyed," by Nancy C. Anderson. © 2003. Used by permission.

"From the Inside Out," by Durlynn Anema-Garten. © 2003. Used by permission.

"What Do You Think?" by Carol Baker. © 2003. Used by permission.

"You Are God's Workmanship," by Betsy Barber and Michelle Lee. © 2003. Used by permission.

"Anchor in the Storm," by Lisa Beamer, taken from *A Reason for Hope in a Time of Tragedy,* © 2001, adapted from pages 9–11. Used by permission of Crossway Books, a division of Good News Publishers, Wheaton, Illinois 60187. www.crosswaybooks.org

"Important Things in Life," "No Room for Lukewarm Christians," "God Has a Plan for Me," "Ready for Heaven," by Misty Bernall. Reprinted with the permission of Simon & Schuster from *She Said Yes* by Misty Bernall. © 1999 by Misty Bernall.

"Guess Who," "Neither Here Nor There," "Gnats and Grace," "What Matters Most," "What a Concept!" "A Sweeping Victory," "Who Wants to Be a Gazillionaire?" "Free Means Free," "Wrong Turns," "The Greed Need," "You What?!" from *If the Tongue's a Fire, Who Needs Salsa?* by Martha Bolton. © 2002 by Martha Bolton. Published by Servant Publications, P.O. Box 8617, Ann Arbor, Michigan 48107. Used with permission.

"Managing God's Stuff," by Joyce Miriam Brooks. © 2003. Used by permission.

"God's Glory," by Carrie Brown. © 2003. Used by permission.

"Seeing Both Sides," by Dianne E. Butts. © 2003. Used by permission.

"Silence and Solitude Are a Frame of Mind," "Surrender Is the Beginning of Peace," "Thankfulness Is a Choice," "Beauty Is More Than Skin Deep," by Deirdre Cantrell. © 2003. Used by permission.

"Sticks and Stones," "Pressing On," by Jane Carr. © 2003. Used by permission.

"Be an Encourager," "What a Rush!" by Kelly Carr. October 27, 2002 and October 20, 2002. Appeared first in *Encounter*, Standard Publishing. Used by permission.

"Fly Boys," by Mary Crist. © 2003. Used by permission.

"When Being 'Nice' Means Not Being Nice!" "Holes in Our Hearts," "In the Yuck of Life," by Shelly Cunningham. © 2003. Used by permission.

"Give Him Praise," adapted from *Certain Peace in Uncertain Times* by Shirley Dobson. © 2002 by James Dobson, Inc. Used by permission of Multnomah Publishers, Inc.

"Press On," "My Identity," by Tina C. Elaqua. © 2003. Used by permission.

"Love Creates Good," "Surrender," from *The Path of Loneliness* by Elisabeth Elliot © 1998 and 2001 by Elisabeth Elliot. Published by Servant Publications, P.O. Box 8617, Ann Arbor, Michigan, 481–87. Used with permission.

"Two Are Better Than One," by Dyanna Espinoza. © 2003. Used by permission.

"Making Room for God," by Andrea Frankwitz. © 2003. Used by permission.

"Truth or Dare?" by Cherie Fresonke. © 2003. Used by permission.

"Death Blow," "My Guy," "Feeling Like a Nobody in a Somebody World," "Yes, Lord!" by Debbie Graham. © 2003. Used by permission.

"A Lesson in Humility," "Resourcefulness," "Encouraging Others," by Diane Guido. © 2003. Used by permission.

"The Advice Column," by Mabel Hale. Public domain.

"Five Golden Rings," "My Strength and Song," "Beauty in the Eye of the Beholder," "Truth or Consequence?" "The Piano Recital," "Marvelous Plans," by June Hetzel. © 2003. Used by permission.

"Wardrobe Check," "Spiritual White-Out," "Five Ways to Make Your Day," "Free to Cry," "Use the Momentum," by Barbara Johnson. Taken from *Joy Breaks* by Barbara E. Johnson, Patsy Clairmont, Luci Swindoll, Marilyn Meberg. © 1997 by New